FEDERALISM IN THE
SOUTHERN CONFEDERACY

FEDERALISM IN THE
SOUTHERN CONFEDERACY

By Curtis Arthur Amlund

Public Affairs Press, Washington, D. C.

INTRODUCTION

Conceivably, every war has within itself economic, social and political forces which make for a centralization of power by the government that gives national direction to the contest. It seems to me that the southern experience during the Civil War gives emphasis to the applicability of this generalization, for in the Confederacy the power of government at the center of the political process was strengthened considerably. The result was that the "sovereign" states had to defer to the concentration of "national" powers by the Richmond government.

Back in the 1920's Frank L. Owsley contended in a book devoted to the subject of states' rights in the Confederacy that the governmental system was destroyed through adherence to these rights. His position was that preoccupation with such rights so obstructed prosecution of the war by Richmond that the Confederacy failed. My own view, however, is that, despite their firmly held states' rights beliefs, southerners were compelled by wartime exigencies to increase the powers of the central government far beyond what was intended originally. And in this on-going process of change a governmental system evolved that revealed a striking resemblance to the one from which the South had withdrawn.

The effort is made in the following pages to find answers to these questions, among others: How did the Confederacy differ from the Union in theory? Was constitutional theory one matter and practice another? Did the individual states retain their sovereignty in full? Did wartime conditions make a difference in the constitutional framework? Did the South have a "national existence"? Was this union a union of sovereign states or a union of the people as a whole? In examining these questions emphasis is put on the nature of relations between Richmond and the state governments, because it is only in gaining a perspective of these relations that answers to specific questions can be found.

In this study particular attention is given to the debates which took place in the Confederate Congress, the opinions of the Confederate Attorneys-General, the statutes at large of Congress, the official Journals of Congress and the Official Records of the Rebellion.

v

The latter works, published by the Government Printing Office in Washington more than fifty years ago, offer several volumes in understanding the functioning of the Confederate government.

The obligations I have to others are many, but I wish to give a special word of appreciation to three members of the University of Minnesota faculty: Rodney C. Loehr, Department of History; the late Asher N. Christensen and Lloyd M. Short, Department of Political Science. An appreciative note is also due John Avery Bond, Associate Professor of Politics, and Dean Seth W. Russell of the College of Arts and Sciences, North Dakota State University, for their expressions of support.

CURTIS ARTHUR AMLUND

ternal to the affairs of the states; on the other side are those who hold that the Civil War amendments were written into the Constitution to ensure protection for the rights of Negro citizens and for those of disadvantaged national citizens generally.

That the conflict of opinion concerning the nature of our system is still with us in the 1960's is obvious. As is explained in these pages, a similar dichotomy of beliefs between supporters of the central and state governments took place in the southern Confederacy in a substantially different context.

Although formal genesis of the Confederate States of America occurred in 1861, the political tenets underlying its evolution reach back to an earlier period of our history. Most ideological cleavages that result in transformations of the political process have a long development, and these transformations are replete with evidences of antipathy whose working within the social, economic and political milieu of a people makes difficult a compromise of divergent viewpoints.

Our Civil War experience provided no exception to the general proposition; antebellum southerners devoutly believed their analysis of the origin of government under the Articles of Confederation and the 1787 Constitution was valid. Their point of view was defended by John C. Calhoun and others who held definitive ideas concerning the nature of the federal system. At the same time the opposing or nationalist point of view was supported by such persons as Justice Joseph Story of the United States Supreme Court and Daniel Webster.

In undertaking a discussion of the constitutional nature of the American governmental system certain questions are in order: What was the status of the thirteen colonies before the Revolutionary War? Did the colonies become independent sovereignties when they declared themselves free in 1776? Were the states sovereign entities under the Articles of Confederation which lasted from 1781 to 1789? Did a union of people rather than one of individual states exist before 1787? Was the 1787 Constitution a compact among state sovereignties or a union of the whole people? All of these questions have taken on a familiarity by succeeding generations of scholars who have retraced our governmental past.

Because there is historical evidence to sustain the arguments of both sides to these questions, the twentieth-century political scientist has to be circumspect about giving validity to data favoring either position. At the most basic level of understanding we are not positive about the exact meaning that eighteenth-century leaders attached to "sovereignty."[1] Although accepting the term as referring generally to supreme

CONSTITUTIONAL BACKGROUND

Throughout most of American history there has been a fundamental divergence of viewpoint about the nature of our governmental system. Although the question of state sovereignty was resolved, at least constitutionally, by the Civil War, controversies over the respective powers of the national and state governments continue into the 1960's.

There has been a resurgence of states' rights opinion since the school desegregation decision of the United States Supreme Court more than a decade ago. During the 1962 confrontation between the nation and Mississippi concerning the admission of a Negro student to the state university, the public was reminded again of disagreement between supporters of national responsibilities and those of states' rights. The latter continue to maintain that the Court has encroached unconstitutionally on the reserved powers of the states—i.e., those powers not granted the national government by the 1787 Constitution.

One conceptual difficulty that inheres in such a question is that the interpretive content of these reserved powers changes from decade to decade owing to the existence of new contexts of problems common to the nation as a whole. Demonstrably, the states' rights viewpoint has been used to inhibit the carrying out of national responsibilities under the equal protection and due process clauses of the fourteenth amendment. In particular the equal rights of a minority people have been frustrated until the recent passage of civil rights' legislation by Congress.

The issues of school desegregation, extension of equal treatment to all citizens using facilities in interstate commerce, equality in voting rights, nondiscriminatory selection of court jurors, protection given by the national government to those who participate in lawful demonstrations in their capacity as United States citizens, labor-management relations, reapportionment of state legislatures and Congressional seats —all of these emphasize the nature of the present contest between the central government and the states over the respective powers of each.

As a result of these controversies two defined points of view have been taken: on the one side are those who contend that the national government should not try to mediate problems that are allegedly in-

About the Author

Curtis Arthur Amlund is currently associate professor of politics at North Dakota State University. He previously taught at the Universities of Minnesota, Oregon and Wisconsin.

A Phi Beta Kappa graduate of the University of Minnesota and holder of its doctorate in political science, he has concentrated his teaching and research interests on the Presidency, the Congress, and American political thought.

He has contributed articles to such journals as the *Midwest Journal of Political Science, The Western Political Quarterly,* and the *Southwestern Social Science Quarterly.*

CONTENTS

INTRODUCTION

Conceivably, every war has within itself economic, social and political forces which make for a centralization of power by the government that gives national direction to the contest. It seems to me that the southern experience during the Civil War gives emphasis to the applicability of this generalization, for in the Confederacy the power of government at the center of the political process was strengthened considerably. The result was that the "sovereign" states had to defer to the concentration of "national" powers by the Richmond government.

Back in the 1920's Frank L. Owsley contended in a book devoted to the subject of states' rights in the Confederacy that the governmental system was destroyed through adherence to these rights. His position was that preoccupation with such rights so obstructed prosecution of the war by Richmond that the Confederacy failed. My own view, however, is that, despite their firmly held states' rights beliefs, southerners were compelled by wartime exigencies to increase the powers of the central government far beyond what was intended originally. And in this on-going process of change a governmental system evolved that revealed a striking resemblance to the one from which the South had withdrawn.

The effort is made in the following pages to find answers to these questions, among others: How did the Confederacy differ from the Union in theory? Was constitutional theory one matter and practice another? Did the individual states retain their sovereignty in full? Did wartime conditions make a difference in the constitutional framework? Did the South have a "national existence"? Was this union a union of sovereign states or a union of the people as a whole? In examining these questions emphasis is put on the nature of relations between Richmond and the state governments, because it is only in gaining a perspective of these relations that answers to specific questions can be found.

In this study particular attention is given to the debates which took place in the Confederate Congress, the opinions of the Confederate Attorneys-General, the statutes at large of Congress, the official Journals of Congress and the Official Records of the Rebellion.

The latter works, published by the Government Printing Office in Washington more than fifty years ago, offer several volumes in understanding the functioning of the Confederate government.

The obligations I have to others are many, but I wish to give a special word of appreciation to three members of the University of Minnesota faculty: Rodney C. Loehr, Department of History; the late Asher N. Christensen and Lloyd M. Short, Department of Political Science. An appreciative note is also due John Avery Bond, Associate Professor of Politics, and Dean Seth W. Russell of the College of Arts and Sciences, North Dakota State University, for their expressions of support.

CURTIS ARTHUR AMLUND

political authority, we can not say with certitude where it resided between 1776 and 1789. Even in the Constitutional Convention at Philadelphia there were those who maintained that the states became sovereign entities after the War for Independence and others who could not accept such a proposition.

Whatever the merits of the individual positions, J. L. M. Curry, one of the framers of the Confederate Constitution, asserted that prior to the Revolutionary War the colonies were separate and distinct political communities.[2] While this situation did obtain, the freedom of the colonies was limited by royal instructions and by an occasional disallowance of colonial acts exercised through the London government. Parliament regulated trade beyond the boundaries of a single colony; the Crown retained control over war and peace, foreign affairs and the postal system, and the Privy Council exercised appellate jurisdiction over colonial court decisions.

There were, then, two governments whose actions affected the individual lives of the colonists, one being the colonial government and the other the London government. It was, of course, the latter which retained the powers of external sovereignty: this is to say that London could make war and peace, conduct foreign relations for the colonies as a whole and use armed force against an outside enemy. That these initiatory developments influenced later political leaders who participated in the formation of the Confederation Articles and the 1787 Constitution was clear.

Another part of Curry's belief pattern was the idea that the Congresses of 1774, 1775 and 1776 retained no genuine governmental powers since they "seldom assumed to go beyond deliberation, advice and recommendation." Contending that the Congresses never pretended to have authority to act on individuals, he emphasized that in all Congressional acts reference was made to the colonies and not to the people—individually or as a "nation." To support Curry's opinions would be difficult in view of the Supreme Court's decision in the *Curtiss-Wright Export Corporation* case, in which the court pointed out that even prior to the Declaration of Independence the colonies acted unitedly in foreign affairs through the instrumentality of the Continental Congresses. These assemblies exercised powers over the issue of war and peace, provided for an army and navy, and adopted the Declaration itself. None of these powers was exercised by a single colony; their exercise was made dependent on what was accomplished by a common agency of all the colonies.[3]

In opposing nationalist opinion, Curry contended that each colony became free and independent in 1776 and had full power to do all "acts and things which independent States may of right do." According to him, the 13 distinct, sovereign republics which emerged from the Declaration formed a "great Federal republic," whose constituent units were the sovereign states. His opinion was shared by the Confederate Vice President, Alexander H. Stephens, who averred that the states became independent on promulgation of the Declaration, which was "made by the people of each colony, for each colony, through representatives acting by the paramount authority of each colony separately and respectively."[4]

Notable exception to these points of view was expressed by Justice Story, who asserted that the sovereignty of the whole was merged into one during the War for Independence. In his opinion the Revolution was won by the "whole for the whole, and not for the parts separately," and the Declaration was proclaimed by all the colonies acting concertedly for all. Holding that the colonies individually were not legally competent to adopt the Declaration, Story maintained that it was an act of "original, inherent Sovereignty." In his estimation the Declaration was accomplished by the people themselves, for it was they who had the right to change their form of government, and when the old form no longer provided for their happiness, they could organize a new one. What took place through promulgation of the Declaration was that the people of the United States became one people bound together in one national government.[5]

In the *Curtiss-Wright* case, already referred to, the Supreme Court held that after the Declaration the United States exercised "full Power to levy War, conclude Peace, contract Alliances, establish Commerce . . . " Consequently, on separation from England the powers of external sovereignty passed directly from the Crown to the colonies in their corporate capacity as the United States of America. It was, moreover, the Court's conclusion that when Great Britain lost its external sovereignty over the colonies, such sovereignty was transferred to the states as a collectivity. If this collectivity now had full powers of external sovereignty, then the presumption can only be that the "sovereign" states did not have unlimited sovereignty or capacity to act.

2

Curry also differed from the views of Story by taking an opposing attitude toward the origin of government under the Articles of Confederation and the 1787 Constitution. For his part, he contended that the Articles of Confederation was formed by thirteen distinct, sovereign states, since the Articles specifically declared each to be independent and that each retained all powers not clearly delegated to the general government. The first article stated that "each State retains its sovereignty, freedom, and independence, and every power, jurisdiction, and right, which is not by this confederation expressly delegated to the United States in Congress assembled." From Curry's standpoint there could be no mistaking that the individual states were left with their "entire freedom, entire independence, entire sovereignty."

Despite the cogency of his argument, the fact remains that the national legislature under the Articles did have power to declare war, make peace and carry on foreign relations with other countries. If the powers of external sovereignty passed to the United States in 1776, then the presumption must be that they were later transferred to the central government of the Confederation. After 1776 no single state was competent to act as a member of the then family of nations, and this condition compromises the argument that the former colonies were sovereign after the Declaration's promulgation.

Of even more basic consideration is the question concerning the nature of the Philadelphia Constitution of 1787. Did the document represent a compact among "sovereign" states, or did it establish a union of people in their individual capacities? This controversial issue has long perplexed scholars. For all practical purposes the answer came in the Civil War and in Supreme Court decisions; it favors the view that the Constitution established a union of people and not a union of sovereign states.

Such a thesis was unacceptable to articulators of the southern viewpoint. Stephens declared the 1787 Union was not a union of individuals "blended in a common mass" with a "consolidated Sovereignty over the whole . . ."; rather the union was one whose "constituent elements were separate political organizations, States, or Sovereignties." His belief was that "ultimate" sovereignty or supreme political authority resided in individuals who were members of an organized political community—the state, and he could not agree that sovereignty might reside in individuals of any by themselves.

The nationalist thesis was held to be untenable by Jefferson Davis, the Confederate President, who averred that all governments exercised their powers in "subjection to the will of the people." This will of the people, he asserted, was not something expressed in "any irregular, lawless, tumultuary manner . . ." It was rather a "will of the organized political community, expressed through authorized and legitimate channels." In his estimation the only people who established the Philadelphia Constitution "were the people of the respective States, each acting separately and with absolute independence of the other."[7]

Diametrically opposed to this interpretation of the 1787 Union were Story and Webster; in their judgment the "will" to which Davis referred was individual in nature. Their contention was that sovereignty resided in individuals *per se*, whose membership in an organized state was not germane. Webster's own words are instructive here: "But with us, all power is with the people. They alone are Sovereignty; and they erect what Governments they please, and confer on them such powers as they please."[8] It was his belief that the 1787 Constitution was not a compact among the peoples of the sovereign states but a "government proper, founded on the adoption of the people, and creating directly relations between itself and individuals."[9]

Extended controversy has long continued over the precise meaning to be given the Preamble to the 1787 Constitution. Early states' rights advocates like Patrick Henry were perturbed by the language used in the introduction to the document: "What right had they to say, 'We, the people' instead of "We, the States'? If the States be not the agent of this compact, it must be one great consolidated National Government of all the States." Noticeably, the language of the Preamble does not refer to any of the states in explicit terms; what it does indicate is that the Constitution was established by the people of the United States as a whole.

Although the wording of the Preamble suggests the formation of a union of people and not a union of states, Curry declared that the Constitution was the "work of the peoples of the States, considered as separate and independent political communities." In his opinion the states were the true authors of the Constitution and "their voice clothed it with authority," making the central government their agent. Both Curry and Davis were in accord about these facets of the conceptual problem; the latter pointed out that the 1787 state conventions, which met to ratify the Philadelphia Constitution, had full powers inhering not in the people *per se*, but in the peoples of the independent states. Asserting that the convention method was the "highest and most majestic form" by which "organized communities" could adopt a constitution, Davis noted the "monstrous fiction" that the people acted as people in their "aggregate capacity" when ratifying the 1787 Constitution.

For his part, Davis believed there had never "been one single instance of action by the 'people of the United States' in the aggregate or as one body." [10] Since there was no such entity as a political community of the people as a whole, the states entered into the new 1787 compact without having their sovereignty impaired, because they retained it from the Articles of Confederation. It was apparent to him that one object of the 1787 Union was to prevent an impairment of the "integrity of the contracting members"—their sovereignty was to remain intact.

To say that these opinions of Davis were in opposition to those of Webster and his followers is to state the obvious. In his 1830 debate with Hayne of South Carolina, Webster emphasized that in referring to the 1787 Union, southerners used terminology applicable only to the Articles of Confederation. While he believed the Articles government represented a compact, the states as such being parties to the Articles, he held that government under the Philadelphia Constitution was founded on a new basis—"not a Confederacy, not a league, not a compact between States, but a Constitution." This fundamental law established a government, a political entity with its own powers. Because the 1787 state conventions, which ratified the Constitution, directly represented the people, the new government had a more popular basis than the central government under the Articles. The latter were approved by the state legislatures themselves and thus lacked the popular basis given the 1787 Constitution.

That the evidence of contemporary understanding about the nature of the act creating the 1787 Union is contradictory is plain. There are many conflicting statements from and about the framers of 1787; we can not say with accuracy what their "intent" was. It is an observable fact that the Supreme Court has held that ours in a union of individuals *per se*. In the case of *McColloch* v. *Maryland* (1819) the Court maintained that the Constitution derived its "whole authority" from people *per se*. It believed the people were at "perfect liberty" to accept or reject the Constitution, and because they had this liberty, their act was conclusive. As the Court said: "It required not the affirmance, and could not be negatived, by the state governments . . . The Government of the Union, then, is emphatically and truly a government of the people." Chief Justice Marshall observed further: "But when 'in order to form a more perfect union,' it was deemed necessary to change this alliance into an effective government, possessing great and sovereign powers, and acting directly on the people, the necessity of referring it to the people, and of deriving its powers directly from them, was felt and acknowledged by all." In the Court's opinion the Constitution emanated from the people *per se*, and its powers were granted by them to be exercised directly on them. This was an important change from the Articles of Confederation, whose central government could not operate directly on individuals, but had to operate through the instrumentality of the state governments.

3

Down through the decades since 1787, controversy has evolved over the division of constitutional powers between Washington and the states. From period to period the latter asserted their right to nullify Congressional laws they considered inimical to their interests. For instance, the Kentucky and Virginia resolutions of 1798-1799 took the form of nullification resolutions. Supported by Republican leadership, these resolutions were aimed at the alien and sedition acts passed by the United States Congress, whose Federalist members anticipated that through the acts they could suppress political opposition to the foreign policies of the John Adams government.

In more concrete terms, Virginia's resolutions declared the acts to be unconstitutional and urged other states to resist them. Thomas Jefferson, disliking the centralizing potentialities inherent in the acts, wrote the Kentucky resolutions which admonished the Washington government not to usurp states' rights by assuming powers not explicitly given it in the Constitution. It was he who appealed to state nullification of Congressional acts as the "rightful remedy" against federal encroachments on these rights. The Virginian held that the 1787 Constitution was a compact to which each state acceded as "an integral party, its co-states forming, as to itself, the other party . . ." [11] And, "as in all other cases of compact among powers having no common judge," each party could decide on the nature of the "infractions" and the method of redress.

The general import of these resolutions was that the general government should remain strictly within its constitutional limits and that the states could intervene, whenever they believed the government was exceeding the intent of its delegated powers. Since there was no common arbiter above the states, each could decide when the central government had exceeded powers delegated to it by the states. While each state delegated certain powers to the central government for common purposes, it reserved the right to its own self-government. What these early states' righters were apprehensive about was that if the the general government could be the sole judge of its own delegated powers, it might assert claim to absolute sovereignty or supreme power; if the central government did so claim, then state sovereignty would be impaired.

These resolutions were authored by a political leader who espoused the cause of France in its contemporary struggle with England; yet, more generally, they were a protest against the Federalist party, which favored the maturation of an active central government. Because the Republicans under Jefferson's leadership were soon to come to power in Washington, the issue of states' rights disappeared for the time being.

Although the issue lost its prominence at the national level, the states' rights "school" was activist in constructing its dogmas. An early member of the school was a Virginia jurist, St. George Tucker, who appeared to accept James Madison's idea of a division of sovereignty between the nation and the states. He agreed that every state could exercise those "parts" of its sovereignty not mentioned in the 1787 Constitution as "parts" to be used in common with other states; yet he also maintained that the supreme authority called sovereignty resided only in the peoples of the independent communities.

There is no misunderstanding John C. Calhoun's concept about the locus of sovereignty, for he held that sovereignty was indivisible. As far as he was concerned, sovereignty had to be located either in the states (he was not here referring to the state governments, but in the larger sense to the states as organized political communities) or in the nation, but not in both. *Apropos* of this supreme political authority, he said: "Sovereignty is an entire thing—to divide, is to destroy it."

In addition, Calhoun sought to distinguish between sovereignty and the power of sovereignty.[12] To confuse the exercise of the powers of sovereignty with sovereignty itself, which resided in the individual communities, was erroneous, according to him. He pointed out that the states delegated specific "powers of sovereignty" to the general government to be used for the common benefit, but since they alone had sovereignty, they could recover the delegated powers whenever they wished. For example, the national government's delegated power over interstate commerce was only an attribute of sovereignty and did not constitute sovereignty itself.

What Calhoun sought to do was to distinguish between governmental powers and ultimate sovereignty. Governmental power refers to the everyday exercise of power by authorities of government, the taxing power providing one illustration of such power. But a people exercise their sovereignty through the amendatory process, because fundamental law is thereby altered, basic relationships among governments and people being changed. Even if we concede that Washington's control over interstate commerce was only an attribute of sovereignty, the relevance is that in practice such control was plenary. When the government used its power to regulate commerce, it was supreme, and any conflicting state law was of no effect. Already early in the last century the Supreme Court was giving judicial approval to the expansion of federal power in this field.

Also it was Calhoun's belief that the people as an aggregate was superior to any government—federal or state—as its agent. When he referred to the people, he meant those members of a separately organized political community—the state, and he equated the "political people" with the state as such.

According to the South Carolinian, the United States was not a nation, but an "assemblage of nations" or peoples as members of their respective communities, the states. The fact that one of the latter entered into a compact to use a common agent for designated purposes did not detract from its sovereignty. This agent, the Washington government, was to conduct foreign relations and regulate commerce, among other role expectations given it, and for these objects the central government could enforce its authority directly on individuals. Calhoun believed this direct relationship between the agent government and individuals represented a novel aspect of the federal system of government deriving from the 1787 Constitution, since under the Articles of Confederation the central government could not operate directly on individuals. When the federal and state governments exercised their "governmental powers," they were functioning as agents of the sovereign states; therefore, these governments were in the relation of equals and co-ordinates, and each agent had the same relation to the sovereign state—"an agent to be ordered, changed, or abolished at will."

It followed that Calhoun believed that even though the federal government was used jointly by the states, this arrangement would not give it any superior position over the state governments. Yet, demonstrably, the supremacy clause of the 1787 Constitution did grant the federal government a superior status over these governments. Under our federal system as we have come to know it, the national and state governments are not in the relation of equals and co-ordinates; each is autonomous within its own sphere of legitimate action.

Under Calhoun's leadership the states' righters, who favored a rigid interpretation of the federal government's powers, adhered to the concept of state sovereignty. For they were apprehensive that

Madison's idea of a division of sovereignty, not a division of the powers of sovereignty, between the states and nation would provide a "stalking horse for centralization." According to them, if the central government could assert that it had sovereignty *and* the powers of sovereignty, it could exert its powers against those of the states. They believed, consequently, that this development would subordinate the states in the presence of an expansion of federal powers, and they foresaw no limits to power increments given the national government. From their standpoint acceptance of the divided sovereignty theory would disadvantage the south's minority position and threaten the protection of its interests.

Both Jefferson Davis and Alexander Stephens were loyal adherents of Calhounian philosophy. As far as Stephens was concerned, the federal government had no inherent power at all, because its powers were maintained by delegation only—delegation, that is, from the sovereign states. Such delegated powers by their nature could be recovered by the states at any time. Stephens could, moreover, not comprehend how sovereignty could be divisible between the nation and states, asserting that no political body could be absolutely sovereign for any purpose and not sovereign for all. Basically, he belived sovereignty could not be divided by individuals *per se,* apart from their membership in the state as an organized community. It was his opinion that the 1787 Union was a union of sovereign states, which established an "entirely artificial or conventional State or Nation," the federal government. The government came into existence through their joint sovereignties, but had no existence apart from these sovereignties.

The constitutional opinions of Calhoun were fully accepted by Curry, who believed the central government could not be superior to the states and declared: "The Union could not exist a day if all the States were to withdraw their co-operation." In order to inhibit the agent government from encroaching on powers withheld from it, formulation of a concept of state interposition was necessary, according to Curry. Under the idea of interposition the states, above which there was no tribunal, were free to exercise their authority by deploying themselves between their peoples and the central government, when the latter tried to encroach on powers belonging to the states.

Opposing the Calhounian conceptualization of our federal system, Webster maintained that the 1787 Constitution relied for its continued existence on individuals and not on the "plighted faith of the States as States to support it." As he pointed out, the federal government could tax individuals, punish those guilty of treason against it and require military service from these same individuals. In his estimation no closer relations could exist between individuals and their government. Said he about the document: "It is not, therefore, a Compact between States, but a Government proper, operating directly upon individuals, yielding to them protection on the one hand, and demanding from them obedience on the other."

Early in the last century the Supreme Court reached a decision in *McCulloch v. Maryland* that had implication for the future of the federal system. In this case the Court emphasized that whenever the federal government made laws in pursuance of the 1787 Constitution, these laws were the supreme law of the land. The meaning of the decision for the central government was that it would be enabled to be supreme within its own sphere of action, and it was the supremacy clause itself which followers of Calhoun had difficulty in rationalizing away. For his part, Stephens held that the general government could make its laws supreme only as long as its delegated powers were not taken back by the states. His opinion was that because sovereignty resided only in the people of each state, they alone as an organized entity could resume these powers. Supposedly, then, the individual states could provide for their separate armies and independently regulate commerce. But the conceptual problem with Stephens' thesis was that in practice the Washington government was supreme, and it was able to pass laws which were superior to any contrary state laws. If the central government was supreme in practice, then the states did not have complete sovereignty.

As Webster stressed, it was not the state government which declared war, concluded peace or conducted foreign relations with other nations. The Supreme Court itself emphasized years later that these powers would have been vested in the central government, even if they had not been mentioned in the 1787 Constitution. In the *Curtiss-Wright* case the Court designated these powers as the "necessary concomitants" of nationality—i.e., powers belonging to the American people owing to their existence as a national state. If the powers of external sovereignty inhered in the Union as a whole, and if sovereign powers affecting internal matters were given to the general government by the people as a whole, the states did not retain their sovereignty in full. If the Washington government was supreme within its sphere of action, then the presumption can only be that there was in fact a division of sovereignty between the states and the nation. Palpably, there was nothing unique about the 1787 Constitution in the sense that there was any abrupt departure from the past. As we have seen, the concept of governmental dualism goes back to the colonial period when there was a division of authority between Great Britain and the colonies.

4

Prior to 1860 various terms were given to the federal system of government, and they included the following: federal, Confederacy, Confederate Republics, Federal Union. In those years before the Civil War the terms were used indiscriminately, lacking any exact meaning. What the 1861-1865 war did was to give substance to our federal system as we now use that term, for after the conflict the Supreme Court held that ours is an indestructible union of indestructible states from which no state can secede.[13] In the *Texas* v. *White* case the Court sustained the opinions expressed earlier by Webster, Story and others of the nationalist school.

Within a federal system there is a division of political authority between the national government and the state governments, each one of which is more or less autonomous within its own sphere of action. More specifically, we can refer to certain "ingredients" of a federal system. First of all, this system divides power between a general government and constituent governments, states or whatever designation is given them. Further, this division of power can not be altered unilaterally by legislative action of the central government. Another ingredient of this system is that matters given the state governments must be substanial. In addition, the central government should have direct contact with individuals through obtaining authority from them in elections, imposing taxes on them and requiring compliance with its regulations. Then, too, the constituent units should be free to change their forms of government and procedures; moreover, these units should have an absolute constitutional equality with one another.[14]

Keeping these ingredients in mind, we shall now turn to observe if the Confederacy of 1861-1865 met these standards. Did it satisfy the criteria that may be used in determining if the system was "federal" in nature.

5

As they withdrew from the Union, southerners tried to diverse ways to justify their action. Curry maintained that the object in "quitting the Union was not to destroy, but to save the principles of the Constitution." He believed the states in his section had attempted since 1789 to keep the general government "within the orbit prescribed by the Constitution," and contended "It was apparent that the majority, having construed away all restraining limitations, would, by construction and usurpation, annihilate the sovereignty of the States and carry out the sectional and selfish purposes for which the Constitution had been abrogated."

Significantly, there was no claim put forward in the state conventions which ratified the 1787 document that a state could withdraw from the Union. George Mason declared in the Virginia convention that the federal Constitution would be "paramount'" to everything— "After having once consented to it, we cannot recede from it"; yet Jefferson Davis held that the right of secession followed from the partnership nature of the Union. Considering the states as sovereign entities, he believed secession was their reserved right, and contended that by withdrawing they "merely asserted" the right held by the Declaration of Independence to be "inalienable." [15]

According to Davis, his section looked toward the move for separation as a "necessity, not a choice." He himself was concerned about the development of a political school in the north which claimed the Washington government was positioned above the states. In particular he lamented the circumstances under which the creature, the central government, had been exalted above its creators, the states, a consequence being that the principals, the states, were being subordinated to their agent, the federal government.

Pointedly, he commented on the reason for withdrawal from the Union: "After many years of fruitless effort to secure from their Northern associates a faithful observance of the compact of union . . . the Southern States . . . decided to exercise their sovereign right to withdraw from an association which had failed to answer the end for which it was formed." [16] In his opinion the Union "had been perverted by those who, feeling power and forgetting right, were determined to respect no law but their own will." Because the south did not want to be weighed down by the "despotism of numbers," it had to form a new association, which was to be composed of states "homogenous in interest, in policy, and in feeling." [17]

Historically, the south was not the first region to favor secession from the Union, for it was in the Jefferson administration that the New England states, agitated by the Executive's embargo, threatened to secede. But the southern withdrawal represented the first overt effort to severe relations with other states, its leaders contending that since the states alone had sovereignty, they could resume their independent existence after having once left the 1787 "compact." Still, as we have seen, the constitutional possibilities of secession were negatived by the Supreme Court in the Texas decision: on admission into the Union the states are incorporated into the whole body politic; since admission is an act of incorporation, there is no recourse for later withdrawal.

The written works of Davis and Stephens reveal in detail the violations allegedly done to state sovereignty and rights by the north; however, their arguments relate almost exclusively to the slavery question, and one can only conclude that their desire to protect that "peculiar" institution constituted the principal reason for secession. That by 1860 the south was beginning to lose its political control of the Washington government was apparent. A northerner had been elected President, whose party was determined to keep slavery out of the territories. In state government many northern legislatures had held the fugitive slave law passed by Congress to be void.

There were numerous indications of concern about the future political and constitutional status of slavery. For instance, the ordinance of secession passed by South Carolina referred specifically to northern hostility toward slavery. According to Curry, the monetary value of slave property amounted to three billion dollars, and the Postmaster General of the Confederacy declared a whole social-industrial system was being "dangerously menaced" in 1860 by the policies of half the states in the Union.[18]

Aside from material considerations, there was the generally held attitude of the section toward the nature of the Negro as a human being. Vice President Stephens rejected Jefferson's minority-held viewpoint that slavery violated the laws of nature and was a wrong. Said Stephens: "Our new Government is founded upon exactly the opposite ideas; its foundations are laid, its corner-stone rests, upon the great truth that the negro is not equal to the white man; that slavery, subordination to the superior race, is his natural and moral condition."[19]

Although the protective tariff and internal improvement questions had strained north-south relations from decade to decade, Stephens gave only minimal attention to them in his book on the war. Southerners had believed the protective tariff aided northern industry to the detriment of their agricultural economy; yet the United States tariff in effect at the time of secession was moderate—so moderate that most southern Congressmen, including all from South Carolina, had voted for enactment of the tariff measure a few years earlier. It was also asserted that the north had benefited more from internal improvements; yet the Confederate Vice President gave only cursory attention to suggested improvements in the new Confederacy which would obviate this alleged defect in the Washington government.

In assigning reason for withdrawal Curry himself referred to the imposition of the tariff system detrimental to his section, the concentration of the government's financial operations in "one quarter of the Union," and the grant of "inequitable appropriations" for internal improvements. He was perturbed by theories which gave a broad interpretation to the 1787 document, as this interpretation had resulted in the expansion of the federal government's powers to a point unforeseen by the framers at Philadelphia. Furthermore, he believed the general welfare clause of the 1787 Constitution had enriched "one section to the prejudices of the other," and had enlarged the "power, prestige and influence of the Union."

These, then, were the constitutional premises on which the fundamental law of the Confederacy was written: at their center was a belief that the states retained their sovereignty and that the general government was a common agent of them all. In brief, the Confederacy was to be a union of states, but was it in practice?

In subsequent pages the "central government" will be used interchangably with the general government, the Confederate government, the government, the Richmond government, and Richmond.

II

THE CONFEDERATE CONSTITUTION

There were few basic changes made in the 1861 Constitution by the framers at Montgomery, but, then, what they sought to accomplish was the inclusion of certain provisions that would satisfy their states' rights predilections. That there was not any desire to break with the past was manifest, for they had become disillusioned with the 1787 document as it was being interpreted by the nationalists. Davis pointed out once that it was "against the violations of that instrument, and usurpations offensive to their pride and injurious to their interests, that they remonstrated." [1] Then, too, the expectation on the part of secessionist leadership was that by refraining from a severance with the old form of government, it could win border state allegiance.

Supporters of the Confederate Constitution were basically reluctant to make the document differ markedly from that of the Washington government. Even South Carolina and Alabama, two states in the deep south, wanted a convention to found a government based on the principles of 1787. Davis himself admitted the new Constitution differed only "from that of our fathers in so far as it" reaffirmed their "well known intent." [2] According to him, the framers had altered the constituent parts, "but not the system of government." For his part, Alexander Stephens indicated that he would not even attend the Montgomery meeting unless the federal model was used; while insisting that slavery and states' rights had to be protected under express constitutional provision, [3] he wanted to uphold and perpetuate the fundamental principles of the United States Constitution.

One scholar has stated that the "most striking characteristic" of the Montgomery convention was its "admiration" for the national Constitution. [4] Significantly, Curry, a framer of the 1861 Constitution, conceded the federal document was copied with "almost literal fidelity." His contention was that specific alterations were made to remedy the "evils" which had provoked secession; these changes were supposed to expurgate the "vicious interpretations of selfish majorities," and to accomplish the "true ends of the Confederacy."

The Montgomery framers were antipathetic toward the expansive interpretation given the federal Constitution by nationalists who favored a viable, centralized government in Washington; for the southerners believed this nationalist interpretation had positioned the central government on a higher constitutional status than the "sovereign states." That these states' rights advocates at Montgomery should have made certain that the new document would be founded on the sovereignty and independence of each state was inevitable, since they had long held that the Union of 1787 was only a union of states and not one of individuals *per se*. Their belief was that sovereignty could not be divided, and that it resided in states which were independent political entities. Accepting these assumptions, the framers proceeded to establish a political system created by and for the sovereign states.

In theory the Confederate Constitution was not created by the southern people as a whole in their individual capacities; rather it was established by separate peoples as members of their own political communities — the states. Still, the framers wrote provisions into the document that negated the concept of a pre-eminence of such sovereignty. Admittedly, there were departures from the federal Constitution, including those which safeguarded the institution of slavery, but the distribution of powers among the three branches of the central government and the division of powers between Richmond and the states paralleled those of the Philadelphia document.

2

Article one dealt familiarly with the national legislature, which was to consist of a Senate and a House of Representatives, the latter to be composed of members chosen every second year by the people of the several states. In voting for Representatives the electors in each state had to have the qualifications requisite for electors of the most numerous branch of the legislature. As was the case with the United States Constitution, Representatives and direct taxes had to be apportioned among the states in accordance with their respective numbers, whose totals were to be determined by a national census to be taken after the first meeting of Congress and every ten years thereafter. The lower house could select its speaker and other officers, and it retained the sole power of impeachment.

The Senate was to be composed of two members from each state; the Senators themselves were to be chosen by their legislatures. In the event of a tie vote in the upper house the Vice President was given the right to cast a vote. Whereas the House of Representatives had the sole power to impeach, the Senate retained the sole power to try all impeachments.

Each house was made the judge of the election returns and qualifications of its own members; either could expel a member by a two-thirds vote. Members of Congress were privileged from arrest during their attendance at house sessions; in addition, they were not to be questioned in "any other place" for "any speech or debate" made on the floors of the houses. Under constitutional provision no members of either house could be appointed to any civil office of the general government during the time for which they were elected.

The procedure outlined for submitting bills to the President for his approval or disapproval was identical with that found in the 1787 Constittuion; however, he was given the item veto power over appropriation bills. Familiarly, all taxing or revenue-producing bills were to originate in the House of Representatives.

Several changes were made in section eight of the first article; nevertheless, the main outline of powers resembled that of the federal Constitution. More specifically, Congress was granted the power to regulate commerce among the several states and with foreign nations. It could borrow money on the credit of the Confederate States, establish uniform laws on the subject of bankruptcies, coin money, regulate the value thereof, fix the standard of weights and measures, provide for the punishment of counterfeiting and safeguard patents and copyrights. Further, the Constitution granted Congress the power to declare war, raise and support armies, maintain a navy and provide for calling forth the militia to execute the laws of the Confederacy. In order to suppress insurrections and repel invasions, Congress could provide for calling the militia into general service. Under the document the legislature could provide for the arming, organizing and disciplining of the militia, and for governing such part as might be employed by the central government.

To facilitate the execution of these enumerated powers, those outlined in detail, the framers included a necessary and proper clause, under which the legislature could take action to implement the enumerated powers. Since southerners had disfavored the expanded construction given the implied powers of the Washington government, it is interesting that the framers should have included this clause in their own document. What the clause did was to offer again a constitutional base from which powers could be expanded in favor of Richmond. Conditions would evolve that would require use of the clause in order to justify new activities undertaken by the general government.

Section ten prohibited various state actions, such as entering into treaties, alliances or confederations, and granting letters of marque and reprisal. It forbade the states to make anything but gold and silver coin a tender in the payment of debts. Also, they were prevented from enacting bills of attainder, *ex post facto* laws, or laws impairing the obligation of contracts. No state was, moreover, to lay any imposts or duties on imports or exports without the consent of Congress.

Article two vested executive power in a President of the Confederate States, who was to be elected by a college of electors. Each state was to have as many votes as it had Senators and Representatives; Congress itself could determine the time of choosing the electors and the day on which they could vote. In the event of the removal, death, resignation, or inability of both the President and Vice President, the legislature could provide for their succession under law.

The President was made commander-in-chief of the army and navy of the Confederate States and was authorized to head the "militia of the several States when called into the actual service of the Confederate States." As Chief Executive he could require the written opinions of his principal officers in the executive departments on any subject relating to the duties of their respective offices. He was, furthermore, given power to grant reprieves and pardons for offenses against the Confederacy, except in cases of impeachment. In his role as chief diplomat he could make treaties, nominate and appoint ambassadors and other public ministers, provided he had the advice and consent of the Senate. In his legislative capacity the President could give Congress information on the state of the Confederacy and recommend to it such measures as he considered necessary. Even more importantly, he was to see to it that the laws were faithfully executed. This provision can be given a latitudinous interpretation by an executive who assumes an activist role toward the office. Lincoln in particular used this clause in association with his commander-in-chief power to strengthen his own position on the controversial actions he took.

Article three covered the judicial power which was to be vested in one Supreme Court and in such inferior courts as Congress might create from time to time. This judicial power of the general government was to extend to all cases arising under the Constitution, the laws of the Confederate States and treaties made under their authority. It extended to all cases of admiralty and maritime jurisdiction; to controversies to which the Confederate States should be a party; to controversies between two or more states; to cases between citizens claiming lands under grants of different states; and to cases between a state or the citizens thereof and foreign states, citizens, or subjects. Since the framers were states' righters, it is not unusual that they should have declined to extend the judicial power of the general government to cases between citizens of the several states.

In all cases concerning ambassadors and others, and those in which a state should be a party, the Supreme Court was given original jurisdiction; however, in other cases the Court was to have appellate jurisdiction both as to law and fact. Under the Constitution the legislature could provide regulations for such jurisdiction and make such exceptions as it deemed necessary.

Article four included the full faith and credit provision: full faith and credit shall be given in each state to the public acts, records, and judicial proceedings of every other. The citizens of each state were to be entitled to all the privileges and immunities of citizens in the others. No new state was to be established within the jurisdiction of any other; nor could any state be formed by the junction of two or more states, or parts of them, without the consent of the legislature concerned, as well as Congress. Familiarly, the central government was obligated to guarantee every state a republican form of government, protect each against invasion and safeguard each against domestic violence.

Article six contained the clause of supremacy, which was copied verbatim from the federal Constitution: "This Constitution, and the laws of the Confederate States made in pursuance thereof, and all treaties made, or which shall be made, under the authority of the Confederate States, shall be the supreme law of the land." Judges in every state were to be bound by oath to support the Constitution, laws and treaties as the law of the land, "anything in the Constitution or laws of any State to the contrary notwithstanding." In practice this provision gave Richmond the legal justification by which it could exert the supremacy of Confederate authority over the states. Under this provision power accretions were both authorized and exercised; its existence presaged the time when the Confederate Constitution and laws would be given a superior legal status over state constitutions and laws. That the 1861 framers did not appreciate the implication of their decision to include a supremacy clause is plain, for the decision signified that the government could take on responsibilities which would exceed the intent and spirit of the Constitution.

Equally important from the standpoint of sustaining the government's position vis a vis the states was the provision requiring members of the legislatures, executives and judicial officers to uphold the Confederate Constitution. In legal terms all officials were expected to give a preference to the Constitution and actions of the central government. It is not easy to reconcile these provisions with others in the Constitution which stress that the Confederacy is based on state sovereignty and that the general government should remain restrictively within the sphere of action given it.

3

The Confederate Preamble differed markedly from that of the federal Constitution, as it attempted to describe with more precision the legal character of the people who were constituting the new system. It began: "We, the people of the Confederate States, *each State acting in its sovereign and independent character* . . . do ordain and establish this Constitution." Here the objective was to disillusion anyone who might misconstrue the precise nature of the government's origin. In effect it was not the people of the nation as a whole who constituted the new system of government; rather it was the people of each state acting in an independent character. Theoretically, these peoples of the states did not establish a more perfect union, but a new federal government. The term union connotes the incorporation of parts into a whole. The framers of 1861 used, however, the term federal government, suggesting that they envisioned a central government which would serve purposes of general interest to the sovereign states.

In the main text of the document there were departures from the 1787 Constitution. One change intended to protect the states from illegal actions by Confederate officials operating within their boundaries, for under the document any officer of the general government who was resident and acting solely within the limits of a state might be impeached by a two-thirds vote of the legislature. That this provision represented an innovation is certain, but there is no evidence that it was ever used by any state.

The times, places, and manner of holding elections for members of Congress were to be prescribed by the state legislatures; however, the national legislature could alter such regulations except as to the times and places of choosing enators. Under the United States Constitution, Congress could alter these regulations except as to the places of choosing Senators. This 1861 document was more explicit than the older one with respect to the qualifications required to vote for Confederate officials, as it restricted the voting franchise to citizens only. During this period of American history the northern states were extending the franchise to aliens, and one consequence was that the alien vote was proving susceptible to misuse by political leaders for their own ends.

The Montgomery framers, admiring British parliamentary practices, inserted a provision into the Constitution allowing cabinet members to sit on the floors of Congress. Constitutionally at least, members were to be given the privilege of discussing any measures appertaining to their departments, but in practice this provision never resulted in more than constitutional theorizing under the permanent government, because military and political realities prevented its implementation.

Another change from the federal document affected the scope of the President's veto power. By giving the Executive an item veto power the framers anticipated that they would be protecting the government against "extravagance, corrupt and illegal" expenditures. In this instance their objective was to inhibit the attachment of pork barrel items to general appropriation bills.

Because the framers wanted to discourage an increase in activities by the central government, they omitted a general welfare clause from the document: what the omission did was to deny to the Richmond government the right to levy taxes to provide for the general welfare, as the Washington government could do. The framers were distressed by the broad interpretation given the welfare clause by nationalists in the United States government, and they believed the most appropriate technique for avoiding a repetition of events would be to elminate the clause altogether. Constitutionally, then, the general government could impose taxes only to raise revenue necessary to meet its debts, provide for the common defense and carry on the government's work.

In order to prevent the central government from fostering industry through high tariffs, the framers forbade the use of public funds to aid business. It was Stephens himself who had alleged that the prewar federal government had protected northern industry through tariff programs. He contended that because his region had relied on cotton as its principal export staple, it had not benefited from the high tariff policies of some Washington administrations. The Georgian was explicit on this point: "The question of building up class interests . . . or fostering one branch of industry to the prejudice of another under . . . the revenue power, which gave us so much trouble under the old Constitution, is put at rest forever under the new." In any event, the Confederate document did not permit the imposition of duties or taxes on foreign imports for the purpose of aiding or promoting any branch of industry.

In addition, no constitutional provision was ever to be construed to grant Congress the power to appropriate money for any internal improvement to facilitate commerce. The legislature could appropriate funds to provide only for lights, beacons, and buoys, and other aids to navigation on the Confederate coasts. Through this provision the framers responded to their belief that the Washington government, when it distributed money for internal improvements, had discriminated against the south, and they wanted to make certain that the central government of the Confederacy would not have an identical power.

Also, the framers provided that no money could be appropriated from the treasury except by a two-thirds vote of both houses; however, such a large favorable vote was not required if the money was requested by some one of the heads of departments and submitted by the President to Congress. Here the framers' objective was to frustrate a resort to legislative riders attached to appropriation bills. Finally, all bills appropriating money were to reveal the exact amount and the purposes for which intended.[6]

Significant restrictions on the Presidency were written into the fundamental law. One reason for their inclusion was a southern dissatisfaction with Presidential elections under the United States government. It was the opinion of Curry that these elections had become a "gigantic" party struggle and that the party organizations had evolved into instruments that were "despotic, heartless" and controlled by the "manipulation of a few bosses." Wanting to avoid a similar development in the Confederacy, the framers forbade the re-election of the President after his six-year term, their anticipation being that since the Executive could not run for re-election, he would use his office for the national interests.

Another constitutional limitation affected the President's removal power. Not agreeing with Alexander Hamilton that the power to appoint carried with it the power to remove, the framers took a more restrictive view of the Executive's power in this respect. Under the Constitution the principal officers in the executive departments and in the diplomatic service could be removed from office at the pleasure of the President. But conditions were imposed on the removal of other civil officers by the Executive or other appointing officials, as these officers were made removable only if their services proved unnecessary, or if dishonesty or incapacity was involved. Under the fundamental law the President was required to send a report to the Senate indicating the causes for removal action.

Curry was concerned about abuses allegedly identified with the patronage power of the federal Executive, asserting that no "more demoralizing" policy of the Washington government had been initiated. His judgment was that the President's power to remove officials for patronage reasons had contributed to an enlarged executive influence in the government. Because such power could be used to reward political friends and punish antagonists, it had "created an evil which the efforts of the wisest and best" had been unable to "arrest or eradicate." In his opinion the federal civil service had proved to be a "jugglery of words, a vain delusion and a snare." Of course, the framers supposed that since the President would have only one term, he would conduct his office in the general interest, and their expectation was that the "spectacle" of a President's "truckling" to special interests would no longer occur.[7]

The institution of slavery was given clear protection under the Constitution. Congress could, for example, prohibit the introduction of slaves from any state not a member, or any territory not a part of the Confederacy. Of more significance were provisions that forbade the legislature to pass any law impairing the right of property in slaves and that safeguarded the institution in whatever new territories the Confederate States might organize. Inhabitants of the Confederacy were to have the right to take any slaves lawfully held by them in any of the states or territories into the new. Under Article four the citizens of each state were given the right of transit and sojourn in any state of the Confederacy with their slaves and other property.

Another protection for the institution was envisioned in the following provision: "No slave or other person held to service or labor in any State . . . escaping or lawfully carried into another, shall, in consequence of any law or regulation therein, be discharged from such service or labor . . ." This provision was intended to preclude any recurrence of situations that had taken place before the Civil War, when the Washington government tried to enforce the fugitive slave law of 1850. That implementation of the law was less than successful was obvious, for the northern states resisted officials who sought to carry out the letter of the law. Southerners had been perturbed by these actions of governments which attempted to render an act of Congress void.

All of these provisions relating to slavery were intended to establish the peculiar institution on a firm constitutional base. As long as the region stayed in the 1787 Union, it could not be assured of protection for its institution, but under the Confederate document adequate safeguards were present. Neither the central government nor the states could impair the right of ownership in slaves, and these slaves could be taken into the territories without interference from any government. Plainly, the hostility found to slavery in the Washington government was obviated, at least constitutionally.

Several changes were made in the amending process of the Confederacy. Within a federal system it is important that the general government not be allowed unilaterally to alter the division of powers between itself and the states. Under the 1861 Constitution there was no possibility that Richmond would be able to change the division of powers, since the first step in the process, that of proposal, was removed from Congress. The national legislature had to summon a convention of all the states when three of them requested a meeting, and a national convention then had to consider proposals for amendment which would have been submitted by the requesting states. Here the objective was to give continuing protection to minority rights.

The second step in the process, namely that of ratification, remained difficult to accomplish under the document, because a proposed amendment had to be approved by legislative or convention action in two-thirds of the states. A decision about the mode of ratification was to be made by the national convention and not by Congress. Whatever the theory, the point is that no amendments were added to the fundamental law during the course of the war.

A final constitutional change was inserted into article six: "The Powers not delegated to the Confederate States by the Constitution, nor prohibited by it to the States, are reserved to the States, respectively, or to the people *thereof*." In this instance the term thereof was used to reassert that the Confederate States did not constitute a whole people, but rather the peoples of the several states.

This, then, was the fundamental law that provided the constitutional framework under which the Confederacy functioned. It was established in the urgency of conflict and given a practical expansion that altered the premises on which the Confederacy was founded. Although dedicated to states' rights, the framers inserted clauses into the document that were not consonant with their basic tenets. Provisions were taken verbatim from the United States Constitution which negated those in the Confederate based on state sovereignty and a general government of limited purpose. Confederate leaders left the 1787 Union because they believed the federal government was undertaking actions that encroached on states' rights. Yet, ironically, they were to be confronted by a central government which, by using the Confederate supremacy clause, would gain political and constitutional ascendancy over the states.

An effort was made at Montgomery to incorporate into the 1787 document a similarly worded constitution with differently intentioned meanings, but it did not work out well in practical terms. In reality the intent of the Confederate framers evolved into a conception of governmental responsibilities that approximated the conception of Washington leaders. Realistically, the full extent of the constitutional powers given Richmond signified that it would be able to assert itself against the states and exceed the sphere of action outlined for it in the Constitution.

Meeting in February, 1861, the Montgomery convention, composed of delegates from the several states, had two tasks before it: the selection of a provisional President and Vice President, and the drafting of a provisional Constitution. The convention selected Davis and Stephens, and then proceeded to frame a temporary document, which differed minimally from the permanent one that went into effect about a year later.

A committee was then organized to draft a permanent Constitution, which was completed by the group, approved by the provisional Congress, composed of delegates to the Montgomery convention, and submitted to the states for ratification. Formal approval of the document was assured upon the endorsement of conventions in five states.

Presidential and Congressional elections were held in November, 1861, and another Congressional two years later. In the Presidential election under the permanent Constitution the electors (each state had as many electors as it had Confederate Senators and Representatives) cast their votes unanimously for Davis and Stephens, neither of whom had a rival for his office under the premanent government, which began to function in February, 1862.

JEFFERSON DAVIS AS PRESIDENT

Long identified in his political and military careers with the Washington government, Jefferson Davis hesitated to transfer his allegiance to a southern government. His initial attitude explains his later behavior as a southern nationalist, affecting as it did his conduct of the office of President. As the Executive he undertook centralizing actions which were stimulated by military events and a personal inclination to follow political practices learned in federal service. The result was that by 1865 he had become a catalytic agent in promoting a concentration of powers at Richmond.

Davis spoke nostalgically of his service under the United States government, confiding that "if future preferment had been the object, it would have led" him to "cling to the Union as long as a shred of it" remained.[1] That he reluctantly became Confederate President was evident, for he admitted: "When the suggestion was made to me, I expressed a decided objection, and gave reasons of a public and private character against being placed in that position."

The Mississippian was not among those who advocated immediate secession in 1860.[2] A Confederate Senator, Clement C. Clay of Alabama, acknowledged that Davis did "not take an active part in planning or hastening secession"; in Clay's judgment the President "regretfully consented to it, as a political necessity for the preservation of popular and State rights . . ." These rights, according to Davis, were threatened by the success of a sectional party, the Republican, whose members were "pledged to make war" on the south.[3] In correspondence dated late in 1860 Davis urged caution in seceding from the 1787 Union and advised against a precipitate withdrawal until the south could move unitedly. "The idea that Mr. Davis was so extreme in his views is a new one," declared John A. Campbell, a Mississippi member of the United States Congress, who said: "He was extremely conservative on the subject of secession."[4]

Because a new government was being established when it was not known if other states would secede, Davis' selection as provisional President by the Montgomery meeting was made in an uncertain political milieu. The politics of the situation required that the executive office be filled by an individual with moderate views toward withdrawal. The reasons for favoring moderation were twofold: it was hoped that the upper south could be enlisted for the cause of states' rights, and it was not foreseeable at this early period how demanding the conflict with the north might become. Curry's contention that there was "no electioneering, no management, no bargaining" in connection with the choice of Davis is unsupportable. Interest in several other candidates was amply evident; Robert Toombs of Georgia was a formidable rival.[5]

Importantly in terms of the evolving federal system, Davis' own candidacy was voted upon by voters living within the states. What this development affirmed was that he did not represent the states *per se;* rather he represented individual voters from whom he gained electoral approval. His accession to the Presidency was not made contingent on his gaining the consent of the sovereign states.

To presume that the Confederacy of a century ago was monolithically favorable toward succession would be mistaken, because the region was a "country" whose people held diverse views on the subject of withdrawal from the 1787 Union. There were variegated opinions held along an extended political spectrum that represented various gradations of states' rights and Whig opinion. Present on the one side of the spectrum were the Whigs, many of whom had supported the Bell electors in the 1860 Presidential elections. These were leaders who did not wish to sever political and economic relationships with Washington. Present on the other side of the spectrum were the "fire-eating" secessionists led by William Yancey and Barnwell Rhett. But between these two groups of opinion-makers were moderates who recommended a more judicious handling of the sectional controversy— Davis himself was one of their articulators.

Acquainted from his Washington experience with the politics of cabinet selections, the President chose cabinet heads who represented different geographical areas in the new system. In order to serve as a political broker, he had to compromise factions; his objective was to gain the optimum political advantage for his new administration. One scholar has pointed out that in making his choices "political availability, not merit, was the determining factor." Under the political environment obtaining in 1861, Davis' course of action was pragmatic; moreover, it was necessitated by the need to inhibit future dissensions in the new governmental system. Since the move for independence involved an intricate change in economic, social and psychological relationships within society, Davis' success as Executive made it essential that he secure the cooperation of those who led opinion-making groups.

In analyzing the composition of the cabinet, Coulter has asserted that "surprisingly enough," the body "little represented the old native planter aristocracy." A possible explanation lay in the satisfaction achieved by the planters when secession did become a fact and not just a theory: after all, their interests were at least momentarily protected and their political demands met. The President did not need to give them any special consideration, as he could anticipate their support.

While six of the Confederate cabinet members had been in the United States Senate and five in the House of Representatives,[7] none had ever served in executive positions in Washington.[8] Only Davis could point to administrative experience he had gained as Secretary of War under Franklin Pierce.

2

In his role as chief administrator Davis assumed an attitude toward his appointing power that conformed to the prevailing ideas of the 1861 framers, who believed restrictions had to be put into the document to prevent a chief executive from making appointments for reasons of patronage alone. In Davis' own judgment the power of appointment constituted a "public trust to be exercised for the public welfare," and he believed the power should not be used as a "private fund with which to discharge personal obligations."[9] Constitutionally, the President had to provide cause for the removal of officers other than department heads and diplomatic personnel. Removals by him had to be reported to the Senate, together with the reasons for dismissal; still, there was a hiatus between theory and practice, as Davis was slow in reporting removals to the chamber and would often make no mention of the explicit reasons for discharge.[10]

Criticism was made of some of his civil and military appointments; yet Davis appeared unconcerned about newspaper and public captiousness. Relying on his constitutional prerogatives, he retained those individuals against whom complaints had been made; however, the question is whether it was prudent for him to keep in office those who had incurred public disfavor for varied reasons. That Davis had to safeguard his constitutional rights is obvious, but it is debatable whether he was able to build political support for his administration by remaining inflexible in these respects.

Party allegiances were minimized during the war and distinct parties as such did not exist. The obfuscation of prewar party alignments could have had an adverse effect on Davis' appointing power, if the assumption is made that the result was an inability on his part to use the power in obtaining party loyalty in Congress. Yet there is no evidence to indicate that the absence of party organizations worked to his detriment. At times his nominations were delayed in the Senate, "but the custom did not become chronic." Even late in the conflict his civil nominations were being sent through the chamber without opposition, although his military nominations were rejected on occasion. When the number of Confederate military defeats increased, Congress did become apprehensive about the President's judgment in the making of these appointments.

Because he would not be deterred by Congressional wishes in nominating individuals to office, he was unable to establish rapport with the national legislature. In one instance the Executive sent to the Senate the nomination of a person to be the postmaster of Montgomery, Alabama; inopportunely for Davis, the nominee had incurred the personal antipathy of William Yancey, the state's influential Confederate Senator. When the latter opposed the nomination, the President responded: "Nor will I consent to be influenced in the exercise of the appointing power which I hold as a trust for the public good, by personal favor or personal resentment." Concomitantly, he declared that the Senator formed "no part of the nominating power." While he would accord the "highest respect" to the opinions of Senators in making nominations, he indicated he would not "yield to any dictation from" them on the subject.[1] The Executive was within his constitutional prerogative here, but it might have aided him politically if he had become less rigid in dealing with Congress. Since he accepted the doctrine of a rigorous separation of legislative and executive powers, the Mississippian was not able to readjust his behavior patterns. It seems reasonable to assume that the appointment of individuals recommended by members of Congress need not have compromised his sense of integrity, for he might have benefited his administration by combining his concern for personal and official honesty with more political sophistication.

3

It was in the ongoing process of administration that problems increased in complexity. For instance, Davis discovered he could not use the Vice President's services to the advantage of his administration, for Stephens appeared detached from governing realities. The Georgian's importance either to the President or to the cabinet proved to be negligible, and when the Confederate capital was moved from Montgomery to Richmond, personal and official relations between the two leaders became strained irrecoverably. Under the Constitution the duties of the Vice President were miniscule, and Stephens, who had been reluctant to leave the 1787 Union, just could not adjust to the new environment.

Predictably, as Richmond began to exercise the constitutional powers given it, Stephens was distressed by the government's efforts to centralize power. In particular he believed the introduction of conscription would lead to a power aggrandizement by the central government and to the diminution of individual liberties. Said he about the conscriptive power: "If compulsion had been necessary at that time . . . the war ought to have been immediately abandoned upon the disclosure of the fact . . . no people are worthy of liberty . . . who have to be compelled to fight." Stephens, removed from actual governing responsibilities, found it easy to be a critic of the administration, but Davis had responsibilities that were primary and urgent.

The problems of administration were compounded owing to several changes made in the cabinet, the offices of Secretary of War, Attorney General and Secretary of State being especially affected. Under a presidential form of government the executive's responsibility for the departments is indivisibly fixed; when cabinet heads are unable to cooperate with him, he has no alternative except to relieve them of their duties. In his capacity as President Davis could not condone actions by secretaries that compromised his own position, since he alone had to be the judge of the propriety of their activities.

There did occur a difference of opinion about the effectiveness with which he managed his official advisers. Early in the war Secretary of the Navy Mallory complained that he would digress in cabinet discussions; the cabinet head opinionated that the "amount of business accomplished bore but little relation to the time consumed." Later, the Secretary revealed that Davis would make military appointments and initiate actions without consulting his cabinet, although Mallory admitted the President was at a vantage point from which he could see "the largest view" and that he did "all for the best." [12] Postmaster General Reagan averred that when "a subject came up for consideration, if important, his (Davis') habit was to exhaust all available sources of information before reaching a conclusion." [13]

Usually, the Executive sought the counsel of his cabinet and urged its members to establish their points of view. In the making of policy Reagan would frequently oppose the prevailing consensus of the cabinet; however, his opposition was consonant with the President's belief that cabinet members should express themselves. That Davis did consult the cabinet on important occasions is evident, for he did so when he selected a new Secretary of War to succeed Randolph, when he sent General Lee northward in 1863 and when he considered peace terms negotiated between Generals Johnston and Sherman. The cabinet agreed unanimously that General Johnston had to be relieved of duty when he staged a withdrawal from northern Georgia in 1864.

Davis' relationship with his cabinet needs to be held in perspective, because from the beginning of hostilities the Confederacy was under continuing military threat, which took the form of enemy invasions at its extremities and a continuing blockade. Constitutionally, it was not incumbent on Davis to consult the whole cabinet on all issues, for he had to take the "large view" on substantive matters before the government.

In trying to gain a general perspective the President necessarily had to focus his attention on the War Department, whose success or failure would determine whether the new governmental system could be established. Since he had served as Secretary of War in the Washington government, he considered himself qualified to supervise the prosecution of the war.[14]

From the outset of the war the Davis administration encountered a variety of harsh realities. Its major reality was a northern threat in Virginia, where enemy presence required the government to concentrate resources in men and material. One result was a paucity of resources for western campaigns, and the policy implication for the administration was that it had to move with great caution. Moreover, the Confederacy did not have adequate men and material to maneuver in force at every point of contact with the Union army; clearly, its forces could not confront federal troops on the basis of numerical equality. Each new northern attack had to be met at the apex of maximum danger, whether it was Fredericksburg, Shiloh or Cold Harbor.

Under these circumstances policy differences evolved between the President and his Secretaries of War. Both James Seddon and George Randolph urged larger military operations in the west, but Davis knew he had to take the large view and he could not subscribe to their ambitious programs. At the same time the Executive had to take

the generalist view of a congeries of situations, he found himself in
the position of having to make successive decisions on the basis of
tactical rather than strategic thinking.

One scholar has suggested that Davis, "increasingly conscious of the
desperate urgency of the Confederacy's plight, took more and more
upon himself." [15] It is difficult to comprehend how it could have been
different, for the Executive's responsibility had an immediacy about it.
The Mississippian might have been too rigid in insisting on his right
to make military decisions, but his constitutional position was defensible.

Cabinet difficulties were complicated by the independence of Secretary of War Randolph, who in late 1862 authorized General The-
ophilus Holmes, commander of the Trans-Mississippi department with
headquarters at Little Rock, to move across the river and take charge
of combined operations on the east side of it. In this instance an
order of strategic importance was issued without the approval of Davis,
who proceeded to reprimand the cabinet officer, declaring that his
policy was that each department commander should remain within
his own army command. He then informed Randolph that "all matters
relating to military strategy and the selection of commissioned officers" were to be referred to him before decisions were made on them.
Randolph might have "had little part in developing military plans";
yet it was the President's prerogative to determine how far cabinet
heads could go in programing military effort.

Owing to the conditions of war the Executive's relationships with
the Treasury, Navy and Post Office departments were limited; these
agencies represented, palpably, functions of less urgency to Davis.
Relations between the President and Navy Secretary Mallory were
cooperative; the latter was given more discretion over the control of
navy forces than was his counterpart in the War Department.

Davis' cabinet secretaries served the President in a familiar role
conceptualization by moderating criticism that in their absence would
have been directed toward him. Congress tended to be critical of the
Secretaries of War, Navy and the Treasury, and the Postmaster General, but "unwilling to sacrifice to popular clamor men who had served
their country faithfully and well," the Executive assisted each department head as he was made subject to legislative displeasure. [16] When
Congress expressed apprehension about Judah Benjamin for his role
in the Roanoke Island defeat, the President transferred him to the
State Department.

The relations of Davis with Congress were not improved by circumstances leading to the resignation of Secretary of War Seddon. Late in the conflict the Virginia delegation in Congress requested that the cabinet be reorganized, and the Secretary, considering the request an adverse reflection on his performance in office, withdrew from the government. In writing about Seddon's retirement, Davis referred caustically to the legislature's action: "I cannot . . . recognize the propriety of your decision, because I cannot admit the existence of a power or right in the legislative department to control" cabinet tenure. Emphasizing that all cabinet members served at his pleasure, he averred that legislators could not determine who should be removed from departmental office, and he affirmed that a legislature-enforced change in the cabinet could not alter the government's policies.

Commenting further, Davis labeled as "unfounded" any "notion" that a Congressional expression of a lack of confidence in the executive branch constituted an "appropriate exercise of constitutional power." According to him, the final responsibility for administration rested with him, and he suggested that if the House of Representatives wanted the issue to be concluded, it could initiate impeachment proceedings against a department head. For his part, he would not countenance a vote in Congress as "requiring concession from a coordinate department of the government." [17]

Despite the 1861 Constitution's adoption of specific parliamentary features, cabinet members were not allowed to sit in the national legislature under the permanent government. That the legislators thought the allowance of seats to cabinet heads would give the executive branch an inordinate political advantage was clear. At one time a bill to permit members to speak on the legislative floors was submitted, but legislators were then preoccupied with overseeing the defense of Richmond, and no action was taken.

It seems plain that Davis exerted a controlling role in the decision-making process that was part of his administration. Although the cabinet did not function as a prominent policy-deciding body, it gave the President the instrument by which he could implement national policy goals.

4

Davis was scrupulous about adhering to the constitutional separation of powers among the executive, legislative and judicial branches, and he resisted Congressional encroachments on his powers. But the President did not allow his own interpretation of his constitutional

duties to warrant his taking any kind of action in the interest of pre-
serving the country. In this respect the Mississippian was not found
in company with Lincoln, who took an enlarged view of his powers as
commander-in-chief and chief executive.

In the absence of legislative authorization the northern President
presumed he had war powers: he suspended the writ of habeas corpus,
made new rules for the armed forces, increased the Union's military
strength and proclaimed the Emancipation Proclamation — all without
consulting Congress. To justify his taking new powers in emergencies,
Lincoln combined the commander-in-chief clause with the take care
provision of the 1787 Constitution to assume that he possessed the war
power. Such a power was to be used in order to sustain the national
interest as he interpreted it to be.

Although Davis did not give a similar interpretation to powers
granted him in the Confederate Constitution, he did protect his prerogatives within the context of executive responsibility as he saw it.
The Constitution also made the Executive commander-in-chief of the
armed forces and obligated him as the head of government to take care
that the laws be faithfully executed. In practice the differences between Davis and Lincoln with respect to their willingness to resort
to the war power were not matters of substance but of degree only.

In his April, 1861, message to Congress, Davis referred to the fact
that Lincoln had taken unilateral action in increasing the armed forces
of the United States. The Confederate President, responding to what
was tantamount to the north's declaration of war, had had to call on
the states to provide volunteers for the common defense. Such a move
had been taken in accordance with the authority given him by Congress prior to its adjournment. At the new session in April, Davis
pointed out that since the legislature had been in recess, he had had
to authorize the issuance of letters of marque and reprisal, which were
used to harass federal shipping. While acknowledging that only Congress could authorize them, he emphasized that the emergency had
required their immediate use.[18]

All existing evidence indicates that the President sought legislative
approval for every act about which he was constitutionally unsure.
For example, he waited for Congress to authorize suspension of the
writ of habeas corpus; he did not suspend it on his own account and
then seek Congressional approval, as Lincoln did. And in his inaugural
address under the permanent government he criticized the United
States government for suspending the writ and denying civil liberties.
Yet within a short time he also found it essential to recommend its

suspension. "He quickly abandoned his State-rights philosophy when faced with the inexorable realism of war."[20] Eventually, Congress was prodded into passing a bill authorizing writ suspension as the result of successive military defeats at Forts Henry and Donelson in 1862.

In accordance with provisions of this law, the President was authorized to suspend the writ and declare martial law in areas under susceptibility to attack. He subsequently issued a proclamation placing Norfolk, Portsmouth and surrounding territory in Virginia under martial law; its issuance meant the suspension of all civil jurisdiction. He also declared martial law for Richmond and suspended the writ there, civil authorities being replaced by the military. Other proclamations were issued which covered the "exposed and disaffected counties" of northern Virginia and the Charleston area of South Carolina. The point is that in all these cases the President carefully delineated the territories to be covered, and when the need for martial law did lessen, he was "quick to restore the authority of the civil magistrates."[21]

While Davis used such authority with restraint, some of his military commanders in the field proved less moderate, for they would suspend the writ without express authorization from Richmond. In 1862 General Hindman proclaimed suspension at Fort Smith and Van Buren, Arkansas, and General Braxton Bragg placed Atlanta and its nearby territory under martial law. But when General Hebert, commander of the Texas department, declared martial law in effect throughout the state, Davis responded with alacrity. Charging that the General's action was "an unwarrantable assumption of authority" and contained "abuses against even a proper administration of martial law," the President made clear his own displeasure with the military commander.[22] Despite Richmond's issuance of a general order abrogating all proclamations of martial law made by the military without Davis' approval, the government had to give continuing supervision over illegal proclamations.

Concerned about seditious activities, the Executive tried repeatedly to gain extensions of authorization to suspend the writ from Congress, but was unable to secure them. Still, he refrained from suspending any without legislative consent, and he always acted within the limits of constitutional authority as he deemed it to exist.

The Mississippian was dedicated to the American tradition of civilian supremacy over the military, the consequence being that he wanted to exert a predominance in the making of military policy. He vigorously countered any attempt to dilute his powers as commander-in-chief. For instance, he contended that he alone had the power to assign generals their duties: "That trust I have been ready to resign at my country's will; but, while I hold it, nothing shall induce me to shrink from its responsibilities."[23] Late in 1861 Generals Joseph Johnston and Gustavus Smith proposed to cross the Potomac and carry the war into the north, but their project was dismissed by Davis, who believed he could not reinforce the operation without a "total disregard of the safety of other threatened positions."[24]

Serving as commander-in-chief, Davis preoccupied himself with the details of military operations. During the Fredericksburg period the Executive, in spite of General Johnston's opposition, ordered the transfer of a division from Bragg's command to that of another general. Here he became involved in transferring men and changing tactics; however, he alone had to take public responsibility for military defeats.

Davis, exercising his military power under the Constitution, was ready to dismiss high-ranking military officers if necessary. Late in the war he removed General Johnston from command because he was disturbed by the General's withdrawal from northern Georgia. In this case Davis was convinced that the commander's move into open country would eventuate in the loss of Atlanta; furthermore, his attitude was doubtless influenced by General Bragg, at that time in charge of general military operations, who was critical of Johnston. Constitutionally, the President had the prerogative to discharge a field commander whose views were contrary to his own, and his wire to Johnston relieving him of command was unambiguous: ". . . as you have failed to arrest the advance of the enemy to the vicinity of Atlanta, and express no confidence you can defeat or repel him, you are hereby relieved."

The President's activities in the military field were not limited to the overseership of personnel, as they affected programing as well. Davis, believing his urgings to Congress should be accepted as a guide, recommended passage of a conscription law in the second year of the conflict; generally speaking, legislators were amenable to his recommendations concerning the military.

As the war continued, Davis demonstrated that he too could be flexible with respect to constitutional niceties. Under the Constitution the central government was not allowed to use public funds to assist private industry; yet the Executive early supported the government's subsidizing the construction of a railroad line. In his recommendation to Congress, he stressed that Richmond could not wait on "private initiative," declaring that "constitutional scruples otherwise admissible" had to be "disregarded in favor of military necessity." [27] Thus, the 1861 Constitution could also be altered when practical considerations had a paramountcy about them.

The Constitution was challenged again later in the war. In his 1864 message to Congress the President advised against placing slaves into military service, asserting that the white population was adequate to fill the nation's needs. But he did acknowledge that his opinion was subject to change, if the country had to make a choice between using them or becoming subjugated. [28] His own attitude was influenced by General Lee's judgment that military necessity required abandonment of slavery, and by Benjamin's belief that liberation would mean foreign recognition of the Confederacy. By 1865 Davis was maintaining that arguments raised against slave enrollment were "beside the question"; [29] what he was admitting was that military urgencies compelled him to accept the idea of using slaves as soldiers. An opponent of the President's plan was agitated to remark: "We have been denying all along that freedom is a good thing for the negro; yet, now we promise to give him freedom in return for enlistment in our armies." [30] After debating the measure, Congress did pass a bill in March, 1865, which authorized the raising of 300,000 Negro troops but left the question of emancipation to the states.

Resolute on the subject of independence, Davis relinquished his constitutional powers only through armed force. Even during the last days of the conflict he averred that although Richmond, Wilmington and Charleston were captured, the south would remain as "defiant as ever." For his part, "no peace would be made which did not recognize its independence." [31]

It would be erroneous to place a weak or strong label on Davis, as there were too many extenuating circumstances in his case. To state that he did the most effective job he could under trying conditions would be reasonable, for without his resolution the Confederacy might not have lasted as long as it did. One scholar has stated that from the first to the last the "administration of Davis remained strong," and that it "steered a straight course" for independence. [32] It appears demonstrable that the government was as vital as it was because Davis held firm in retaining his constitutional powers.

6

Not surprisingly, relations between the President and Congress deteriorated as military reverses increased in severity. More generalist-minded than the legislature, Davis succeeded, however, in preventing Congress from gaining a superior constitutional status.

That personality clashes contributed to irritations between the branches was apparent, for Senator Clay wrote in 1863 that the Executive "would not ask or receive counsel — he is predisposed to go exactly the way his friends advised him not to go." Apropos of the personality problem, Senator William Simms of Kentucky commented: "We as Congressmen have foreborn and tried to harmonize with the President. His friends have tried to get him to change his policy, give up bad generals, and surrender his favories in the army." [33]

In vetoing legislative bills the Executive was circumspect and favored restraint unless opposition to Congress was called for. Although he vetoed 39 bills, only one was over-ridden by the national legislature. A definition of some of the vetoed measures is now necessary.

Within the area of national affairs the Mississippian was perturbed by Congressional placement of time limitations on the grant of authorizations to suspend the writ of habeas corpus. He argued that a "suspension of the writ when demanded by the public safety" was as much "a duty as to levy taxes" for the government's support. In order to put curbs on subversion, Davis asked Congress late in the conflict to authorize writ suspension; when the legislature resisted, he informed members that they would have to take responsibility for refusing to "exercise a power" to be used in periods of "national peril."

Although a nationalist, the President did not try to remove from the states those subjects long of traditional legislative concern to them. He vetoed one bill under which Congress presumed to pass laws relating to the distribution of estates of deceased military personnel; in his veto message he emphasized that Congress was without power to "change vested rights governed by the laws of the states." [34]

He would not, moreover, approve a House passed bill providing for a general ticket system of election for Representatives whose districts in Tennessee were under federal occupation. In this case his opinion was that any attempt to have members of the House of Representatives chosen by the state as a whole violated the 1861 Constitution. According to him, the national legislature could pass measures pertaining only to the manner of holding elections and not the mode of representation. Just as objectionable to Davis was another part of the bill which intended to prescribe voter qualifications, a right belonging "exclusively to the States." [35]

In later bills both of these features were removed, and the invaded states were enabled to retain their membership in the House. Congress made it possible by providing that Louisiana Representatives from occupied districts could be elected by qualified Louisiana voters living in other parts of the Confederacy. Similarly, qualified Tennesseans anywhere in the Confederate States were given the right to vote for House members; such arrangements were also made for Kentucky and Missouri. In each instance Congress refrained from prescribing voter qualifications, and the legislature in Richmond was careful to make all arrangements contingent on their authorization by the state assemblies.

Whenever Congress tried to encroach on his constitutional powers, Davis proved responsive. Early in the conflict the legislators attempted to create an office of commanding general of the Confederate armies. Considering the measure an attempt to reduce his status as commander-in-chief, the President pointed out in his veto message that the bill granted powers retained solely by the Executive within the meaning of the commander-in-chief clause of the fundamental law. He dismissed the bill as an "inadvertence" on the part of Congress. Constitutional protection of his power was invoked by him on another occasion when he declined to permit a general to "take the field at his own discretion and command any army or armies" as he might unilaterally choose.[36]

The President vetoed, too, a bill which authorized the Secretary of War to receive a regiment of Texas volunteers into Confederate service. Since these volunteers were not to be under the government's control, he had no alternative except to veto the bill, for he could not allow the incorporation of troops into Richmond's armies who could not be supervised by the general government.

Another Congressional measure vetoed by Davis related to the organization of a general staff of armies in the field. Here the Mississippian objected because it gave commanding generals the authority to assign one of their general officer subordinates as a chief of staff. Under the bill such appointments could be made without the necessity of the commanding generals' referring the matter to the War department. Another vetoed measure gave the Secretary of War or commanding general the authority to promote officers, and under the bill no action by the President was contemplated.[37] If Davis considered himself to be commander-in-chief, he had no choice other than to veto the measure.

Near the end of the war the Executive was so troubled by legislative attempts to have Lee made commander-in-chief of the armies that he would not accede to a Congressional request that General Johnston be restored to command. He considered the request an "impertinence" and an attempt by the legislature to arrogate to itself the making of executive policy.[38] Eventually, Congressional pressure in behalf of Lee became intense, and the President believed it essential to acquiesce in a bill establishing the office. In creating the office of commander-in-chief of the armies, Congress stated that its objective was to restore "public confidence" and ensure an "energetic administration of military affairs."[39] In reality it mattered little what legislature did or did not do at this time because it was early 1865.

It seems clear that Davis was a nationalist who could not allow his own sentiments in behalf of states' rights work to the detriment of nationwide interests. Theoretically, he could remain loyal to these rights and the concept of state sovereignty, but he had to give executive direction to the government and put theory into practice.

IV

CONGRESS IN ITS NONFISCAL ROLE

The Confederate Congress was a "weak, spasmodic body," declared E. A. Pollard, a critic of the Richmond government, who asserted that it had "no organization of opinion in it; no leaders, plenty of idle debate, capricious measures."[1] That these are unsupportable remarks is apparent, for they do not stand against an examination of the legislature's performance in office. The Alabama secessionist, William Yancey, once observed that the Congress' record would reveal that it had "not failed to meet the crisis with all the energy consistent with the fundamental character of its organization."[2] Although states' rights in predilection, a majority of members held views conditioned by emergency which sustained the assertion of national powers. A careful reading of Congressional debates reveals legislators who were aware of the demands made upon them in establishing a new system of government.

The tasks before Congress were considerable: in a few short months a central government had to be established, and the legislature had to provide the statutory framework within which the government could begin to function. A complaint made by Stephens that Congress was a "futile body, spending so much valuable time on minor details," seems unjustified because the legislature had to preoccupy itself with those minor details which would give the government the legal bases to implement national programs.

To say that Congress measured up to responsibilities which far exceeded those envisioned for it by the 1861 framers would be accurate. The degree to which the legislature passed measures centralizing powers at Richmond steadily increased, and in diverse areas of decision-making Congress enacted bills whose spirit was in contradiction to the basic character of the general government.

The Constitution itself presented the legislature with the legal foundations for an expansion of powers. Under section eight of article one it was granted extensive powers to carry out national goals, since the legislature was delegated most of the powers conferred on the United States Congress by the federal Constitution. Within this section there was the familiar necessary and proper clause, whose existence meant the legislature could pass measures in order to implement its enumerated powers. Under the Washington experience this clause had been used in conjunction with one or more of the enumerated powers to facilitate an expansion of national powers, and an identical clause enabled the Richmond legislature to give a similar implied expansion to these powers.

Significantly, many members of Congress had been in Washington service as legislators, about one-third having been in the federal body. At one time or another there were 260 individuals who served as members of the Confederate legislature; however, only 10 per cent of the membership continued throughout the war. One serious problem, consequently, was the lack of continuity in experience and service for Congress as a whole.

Out of 26 Senators in the first Congress, more than half had been members of the United States Senate; these former Washington legislators, "men of aggressive temper," formed the nucleus of opinion-makers who advocated the cause of an active central government in Richmond.[4] From their own experience in Washington, they had been initiated into the centralist-decentralist contest which occurred in the United States Congress; subsequently, the nationalist group within the Confederate body carried on the same struggle for Richmond.

Several measures enacted by Congress during the early part of the war evidenced a power displacement to the advantage of the general government. A decision was made to organize a military force representing the Confederacy as a whole. To provide for the common defense, the President was authorized to use state militia called into Confederate service.[5] He was granted authority to take control of such telegraph lines as "to enable him to supervise communication passing through" the country. What this development meant was that he could inhibit the transmission of "any communication deemed to be detrimental to the public service."[6] He was, moreover, authorized to advance money to a railroad company for the purpose of encouraging the building of a branch line essential to the war effort.[7] All of these initial measures had implication for the future because with the passage of time the central government would assume more and more powers to prosecute the war. Varied activities were undertaken by Richmond owing to its constitutional powers to declare war, raise armies and provide for the common defense. In defending its actions Congress could refer to the necessary and proper clause as justification for their legality, thus asserting its implied powers.

That Congressional debates should have centered around various facets of the military programs initiated by Richmond was inevitable, for the legislature was scrupulous about retaining its constitutional powers. In passing legislation relating to suspension of the writ Congress was careful to delimit the President's discretion to suspend it. Under the fundamental law Congress alone could authorize suspension, and only it could decide when the public safety required authorization for suspension. Using its constitutional power, the legislature limited the time of application for suspension, and delineated the categories of offenses that were to be restrained through suspension, for members were determined to see to it that executive authority accompanying the suspension would be restricted to areas under federal attack. An 1862 act, to illustrate, permitted Davis to suspend the writ only "during the present invasion of the Confederate States." [8]

Members expressed concern over the President's occasional resort to martial law, although during a debate in late 1862 Representative Edward S. Dargan of Alabama suggested that there might be times when aggressive action had to be taken. John B. Baldwin, a Representative from Virginia, declared that unless the Executive's "wings" were "clipped," however, Davis might "go to extremes." While a Representative from Louisiana, Charles M. Conrad, believed the President could resort to martial law in cases of necessity, he thought Congress had acted properly in rebuking army generals who had exceeded their own authority in martial law cases. [9]

Long debates focused on the legality of various provisions of the conscription progam. Under it Richmond directly enrolled into Confederate service those persons who were within designated age limits. The first conscript law authorized the President to draft all white men between 18 and 35 years for a period of three years, and to call into service the entire reserve of men not initially needed, if the "exigencies of the public service" should require it. [10]

With respect to the legality of this program Senator John B. Clark of Missouri argued in 1862 debate that the sovereignty of the states had to be secondary to that of the people in "times like these." The Senator was implying that there was a sovereignty of the people as a whole, intimating that the Richmond government operated as an entity apart from the states themselves. His remark pointed to the existence of a centralist-decentralist dilemma which the President and Congress had to resolve by deciding if state or national rights and powers were to be asserted.

A states' rights supporter, Senator Williamson S. Oldham of Texas, held that Congress could not directly force citizens into the Confederate army except through the instrumentality of the states, suggesting that his idea was not "circumlocution" but the "theory of our government." His expectation was that the Confederacy could win the war without violating its own fundamental law, but violation would be done to it if Richmond tried to conscript persons of its own accord. His viewpoint was shared by Representative Baldwin, who contended that Congress did not have the power to conscript men just because the Constitution granted it the power to raise armies. As far as the Virginian was concerned, the state militia constituted the "greatest war power in existence."

Other members of Congress supported the use of conscriptive power by the central government. Ethelbert Barksdale, a Representative from Mississippi, maintained that there was not a single "dissenting voice" in his state against conscription, while W. Porcher Miles, a South Carolinian, averring that he yielded to no one on states' rights, emphasized that the country had to be "saved." A Representative from Tennessee, Meredith P. Gentry, argued that the power of Congress over those of military age was adequate to "meet any emergency" which might develop. Constitutionally, the legislature was given the power to raise armies, and since it could do whatever was necessary and proper to carry out this power, Congress could by implication draft men into general service.

Congressional debate over conscription dealt with multiple aspects of the program. Senator Oldham believed Richmond could not "enter a State and take all the inhabitants"; yet William E. Sims, a Kentucky Senator, thought the legislature could require "the service of every man in the Confederacy." A Georgia Senator, Benjamin H. Hill, pointed out that the war was going to "every man's door alike," maintaining that the conflict gave Richmond the power to take both state citizens and the officers into general military service.[12] His position represented the quintessence of centralist doctrine, the idea being that the general government could demand services from all Confederate citizens.

That legislative debate should have evolved from a discussion of conscription to an analysis of the system of government established at Montgomery was ineluctable, for the conscript program was of direct urgency to Congress and citizens alike. The central government was thought by Senator Edward Sparrow of Louisiana to be "more than a mere agency." He believed the "war power of Congress was unlimited"; yet he asserted that it should be "discreetly exercised so as not to endanger and overthrow the State Governments."[13] A contrary position was taken by Senator Yancey, who stated that the sole purpose of the central government was to defend the "constitutional liberties of the States, and of the people" of the states. Yancey himself could not conceive the existence of a people of the Confederacy as a whole apart from the peoples of the several states. Yet Senator James Phelan of Mississippi thought Congress "could exhaust the population to save the national life." [14] What the Senator was referring to was a national existence apart from that of the individual states.

Legislative discussion about the desirability of creating a Supreme Court led to an intensification of differences concerning the nature of the governmental system. What was contemplated for a high tribunal was for it to resolve controversies between the general government and the states. It was the belief of Senator Phelan that if each state were given the right to decide what Confederate laws were valid or invalid, the central government would cease to exist. [15] For his part, Senator Yancey asserted that the Confederacy had "adopted a great deal too much of the Constitution of the old Government," concluding that if a high court were given appellate jurisdiction over state courts, it "would subvert and destroy the sovereignty of the States." Agreeing with Yancey, Senator Barnwell of South Carolina considered it a "monstrous doctrine" that a Confederate court should have appellate jurisdiction. The opinion of Senator Oldham was that if such jurisdiction were given a Confederate court, the states would be inferior to Richmond. Thomas J. Semmes, a Senator from Louisiana, declared that the "history of the United States supreme court was one of encroachment and usurpation." [16] An antagonist of Davis, Henry S. Foote, Representative from Tennessee, thought a high court would bring the states into "dire conflict with the central government." Whatever the merits of the respective positions, a court was never established.

As the war years continued, the general government did become more involved with the personal lives of citizens living within the states, and it began to affect these citizens through its program relating to the subsidy of private businesses, impressment, writ suspension and conscription.

Because the government wanted to encourage the manufacture of saltpeter and small arms, Congress made money advances to stimulate the construction of the required facilities. [18] Legislative efforts were initiated to increase iron and coal production, and the President was given authority to "enter into contracts for the purchase of coal and iron, in such quantities" as might be needed. [19]

A railroad bill enacted in 1863 gave Davis the power to require "any carrier to devote its facilities to the support of the army"; under the law Richmond could prescribe railroad adherence to through train schedules. By 1865 the central government was no longer threatening companies that would not cooperate with it; rather it was indicating that the government would place the employees of uncooperative roads into military service.

In order to find a constitutional base for these activities, the general government could refer to its powers to declare war and support armies. By using these powers in association with the necessary and proper clause, the government could assume it had the implied power to undertake such activities. The Montgomery framers were disturbed by the manner in which prewar federal Congresses had fostered internal improvements of benefit to the north; yet Richmond soon discovered how essential it was to encourage the construction of factories and railroad lines, and the working of mines.

Despite adverse economic conditions the national legislature was unable to bring itself to pass a general price-fixing law; however, a committee did examine the feasibility of imposing maximum prices on "all agricultural, mechanical and manufactured articles." [21] Even though the proposal failed to win approval by Congress, it is revealing that this kind of proposition was ever advanced, for its implementation would have strained states' rights predilections further.

That Congress should have made no attempt to regulate the growing of food supplies is understandable because such legislation would have resulted in the imposition of governmental controls over agriculture. This was still the 1860s when the scope of governmental activities was restricted, and it would be inappropriate to compare the range and extent of functions assumed by Civil War governments with those of the 20th century. Congress did pass a resolution urging citizens to grow provision crops rather than cotton and tobacco. Augustus E. Maxwell, a Florida Senator, resolved that it was the "deliberate judgment of Congress . . . that the amplest supply of provisions for armies and the people should be the first object of all agriculturists." [22]

During 1864 the government's control over commerce increased through the passage of a law under which part of the cargo space of outgoing and incoming vessels was reserved for the exclusive use of Richmond. The law forbade, moreover, the importation of luxury items, including furs, stones, antiques and carriages. Using its power to regulate commerce with foreign nations, the central government was thus able to exert supervision over foreign trade for a period of several months. To moderate the complaints of states' rights-conscious governors about the severity of Richmond's trade regulations, the government finally withdrew them early in 1865.[23]

The individual lives of Confederate citizens were also affected by an act passed early in the conflict which authorized the Confederate military to "destroy cotton, tobacco . . . or other property of any kind whatever" that might be of aid to the Union.[24] Enactment of this bill signified that the general government could expropriate the property of Confederate citizens under conditions of military necessity.

The relationships between Richmond and Confederate citizens, and between the government and the states were further strained by passage of an impressment law in 1863. Said the language of the law: "That whenever the exigencies of any army in the field are such as to make impressments of forage, articles of subsistence . . . necessary, then such impressment may be made by the officer . . . whose duty it is to furnish such . . . property for such army." [25] Government and state officials were to administer the law jointly, the objective being to determine a fair and equitable price for all material impressed. In effect the law sanctioned the government's seizure of property anywhere in the Confederacy.

In this same year the Confederate military posture began to deteriorate, and Congress responded by enacting a law authorizing the President, Secretary of War and commander of the Trans-Mississippi department to suspend the writ of habeas corpus. This response came after the Davis administration had requested authorization to suspend in order to curb subversive activities, prevent illicit trading with the enemy, and arrest deserters and those persons abetting them. As always, Congress limited the Executive's use of suspension by declaring the authorization would not continue more than 90 days after the next meeting of the legislature.[26]

Late in the war manpower requirements became burdensome, and Congress debated the possibility of even more directly affecting the lives of citizens. It was disturbed by the number of persons who were being exempted from military service on one account or another. Representative John R. Chambliss of Virginia proposed to remove farmers from the exempted list, asserting that he was "unwilling to give preference . . . to one class over another." [27] In addition, the question arose over what to do with those men who had paid substitutes to perform their military obligations. It was Senator Orr's opinion that the government had entered into an unbreakable contract with those who gained exemption by providing substitutes. Yet Senator

Maxwell pointed out that Richmond could not make "any contract exempting a citizen forever from military service," concluding that the "life of the country must be preserved." [28] The legislature decided these contracts were recoverable and forbade the future enrollment of substitutes.

A measure enacted in 1864 made free Negroes between 18 and 50 years liable to perform such duties with the army as the Secretary of War might determine. [29] The same law also looked toward the employment of 20,000 male Negro slaves for work on military fortifications. Finally, just before the end the legislature approved a bill providing for the use of slaves as soldiers. From the standpoint of the philosophy which underlay the Confederacy, it is an anomaly that this measure ever won passage, but by 1865 the time had long since passed when the central legislature would demonstrate circumspection in exerting national powers.

In the last year rumors circulated about peace negotiations, and a question emerged concerning which governments, Richmond or state, should initiate the negotiations. In order to dispel rumors about them, Representative Miles emphasized that since Congress alone could declare war, the general government would have to undertake the negotiations. In his opinion any state attempts to negotiate a peace would be a violation of the Confederate Constitution and would be "revolutionary." [30] Consequently, in making peace Richmond did not plan to serve in a subordinate role to the state governments.

A comment should be made about the nature of membership in the Confederate House of Representatives and Senate. The House did not represent the states as separate entities; it directly represented southerners as individuals, and its members were popularly elected from the same Congressional districts used before secession. As was the case with their federal counterparts, the Confederate Senators owed their election to the state legislatures, thus representing the states *per se*.

V

CONFEDERATE FINANCES

The problems of financing the war were complicated by a federal blockade and the lack of an industrial base. Because the prewar south had had a major share of its assets frozen in land and slaves, there was insufficient capital to build an industrial economy. Its meaning for the war was that Confederate leaders did not have a viable industrial establishment with which to sustain financial burdens.

Manifestly, there was a cause and effect relationship between financial conditions and battlefield fortunes. That military defeats in 1863 should have caused a loss of public confidence in Confederate success was inevitable; still, it is questionable that Richmond could have taken any different course in finance. The economic fact was that the Confederacy just did not have a diversified enough economy to continue large-scale military efforts for an indefinite period.

Under the Constitution the national legislature was granted power to borrow money on the credit of the Confederate States, and early in 1861 Congress authorized the issuance of eight per cent bonds totaling 15 million dollars.[1] The government's assumption that the interest and principal on the bonds could be met by imposing an export tax of 1/8 of one per cent per pound on cotton proved to be incorrect; moreover, the public's reaction to this first bond issue was disappointing, and the amount was not subscribed until November. Full implementation of the law was inhibited by the requirement that would-be purchasers deposit five per cent in specie when buying bonds. Since most banks had suspended specie payment after the conflict began, bond buyers were hard put to find the necessary specie.

The Treasury department soon realized that the bond issue would not bring in sufficient revenue, but it erred in believing the first issue could be maintained by the export tax on cotton. Two factors accounted for the inadequacy of the cotton tax: the Union blockade prevented the shipment of goods abroad, and an informal cotton embargo had been put into effect to solicit foreign recognition of the government.

Realizing that the bond issue alone could not provide enough revenue, the Treasury also floated one million dollars in Treasury notes, which were made payable in a year and bore an interest rate of 3.65 per cent.[2] In practical terms both the bond and Treasury note issues represented short-term measures, because Richmond's large financial requirements could not be met by the small amounts envisioned under them.

Later in this first year of war C. G. Memminger, Treasury head, recommended that Congress authorize a bond issue of 50 million dollars, whose holders were to receive eight per cent interest on their money. The legislature did respond by passing a bill which obligated Richmond to accept from investors the "tender of any resources available as a means of credit," the so-called produce loans. Concomitantly, it authorized the issuance of 20 million dollars in noninterest-bearing Treasury notes, which were made redeemable in specie in two years. Besides, Congress authorized the floating of a 30 million dollar loan in high interest-yielding bonds, which were then made payable at the end of twenty years from the date of issuance.[3]

Through the produce loans Richmond received quantities of cotton, tobacco, sugar and rice, the difficulty being that the government discovered itself with undisposable commodities, since the blockade prevented their shipment to Europe to be converted there into foreign credits. By the end of 1861 only 21 million dollars in specie and produce values had been subscribed under the act.[4]

What these developments meant was that during the early months of its existence Richmond had to finance its operations through the use of promissory notes, which involved a promise on the part of the government to pay its creditors. Wanting to reduce the number of these notes, Congress imposed a special war tax on the states in August, which placed a tax of fifty cents on each 100 dollar evaluation determined for a broad category of property found within the states of the Confederacy. The statute also authorized a bond issue amounting to 100 million dollars, and permitted an increase in the amount of Treasury notes to a similar total. The latter were made convertible into bonds yielding a high interest rate, and they were made receivable for the war tax and for all "public dues except the export duty on cotton." State governments sought to satisfy their war tax obligations by issuing their own bonds and notes, for they found it politically expedient to postpone increased state taxes. That this special tax failed is evident, for by 1863 it had brought in only 18 million dollars.

Throughout the conflict Richmond had before it the psychological task of convincing the public that the war could be won; such a task had at least to be tried in order to maintain financial stability. Although

Confederate money remained at par with gold and foreign exchange during the early months and was at par with gold in late August 1861, the favorable exchange rate did not long continue. While the government's expenditures increased to 165 millions for the first year, its revenues totaled only 1,270,000 dollars: this gap between expenditures and revenue had a deleterious effect on public trust in its fiscal stability.

From the beginning Secretary Memminger anticipated there would not be a "wild inflation" through the issuance of Treasury notes, believing, incorrectly, that the notes would be used to purchase interest-bearing bonds.[5] Equally incorrect was his assumption that the notes in circulation would remain in constant and even quantity. What happened was that the notes were used to buy tangibles, and an inflationary process was initiated from which the Confederacy never recovered.

As the conflict went on, the central government turned more and more to Treasury notes for its operating expenses. The Secretary, unable to gain public response to bond issues, was compelled to issue noninterest-bearing notes, which had no metallic backing. Such Confederate money merely assured payment in dollars to the holder "two years after the ratification of a treaty of peace" with the United States government. While Memminger preferred to issue only interest-bearing notes, Congress favored the non-interest bearing paper, and successive issues of these notes served to inflate prices even further.

For the general government to have assumed that investors would fund their notes for bonds was an optimistic assumption; of course, bonds yielded a higher interest rate than the interest-bearing notes and supposedly paid in specie, but the problem was that Richmond could not meet bond interest payments in specie. In the early period of the Confederacy interest was paid from coin reserves found in the country; however, as the supply of specie declined, interest obligations could no longer be satisfied with hard money. Not unexpectedly, what happened then was that investors lost their enthusiasm for bonds.

Repeated attempts were made by Richmond to stimulate Treasury note holders to fund their notes for bonds; but the noteholders, who believed the government could not meet interest and principal payments on bonds, kept their paper money, and used it to satisfy current obligations and to speculate in gold or commodities. Admittedly, the Confederacy was not alone in believing noteholders would convert their notes into bonds, for the assumption that they would do so "prevailed in the South as well as in the North."[6]

Congress declined to impose heavy taxes on Confederate citizens, since it proved easier to issue notes and bonds than to tax. Any encouragement for taxes was not forthcoming from Vice President Stephens, who contended that the government should make the war "fall as lightly as possible" on citizens.[7] Although President Davis was aware that defense requirements had resulted in large expenditure outlays, he, too, was unwilling to impose burdensome taxes. Because the central government was new, it is comprehensible that it should have demonstrated a diffidence in tax matters; again, Richmond was not alone, as the Union government also revealed an apathy in initiating a tax program whose incidence on the northern taxpayer would be substantial.

Secretary Memminger was not unaware of the importance of relying on taxes rather than loans, but he was cognizant also of the practical difficulties that lay in collecting a direct tax. Fundamentally, the problem was one of public antipathy toward internal taxation, and in February, 1862, the government had to announce that the war tax "had to a large extent proved a failure."[8] It appears there was no constructive alternative to a paper money policy to which Richmond became "irretrievably committed."[9] Following the program of least resistance, Congress increased the number of notes, stocks and bonds issued under earlier acts to 250 millions.

In his message of August, 1862, Davis acknowledged that the public apparently preferred Treasury notes as a circulating medium, and he expressed his approval of the continued issuance of them. His judgment was that paper money issues could be kept manageable: "No grave inconvenience need be apprehended from this increased issue, as the provision of law by which these notes are convertible into . . . bonds forms an efficient and permanent safeguard against any serious depreciation of the currency."[10] In this instance the President was being unrealistically optimistic, because those who invested in government bonds received their interest in depreciating notes whose value was constantly fluctuating.

In the middle of 1861 ten per cent of the total Confederate debt was covered by Treasury notes; yet four months later the percentage had risen to sixty six, and by February of the succeeding year these notes represented seventy-four per cent of the debt. Just as the debt increased rapidly, so did the expenditures of the general government increase precipitously; by the end of December, 1862, its operating costs had exceeded 580 millions.

Although he considered once the possibility of making notes legal tender, Memminger decided that the notes did not need any assistance to "enable them to perform the function of legal tender." In his opinion any law to compel acceptance of paper notes as legal tender would engender distrust of the currency and "shake public confidence."[11] All legal tender proposals considered by Congress were opposed by the Treasury head: his attitude prompted one member to state that he thought it novel that the Constitution could give the government the power to wage war and then "deprive it of the most efficient tool for the purpose."[12] In spite of the Congressman's opinion the legislature as a whole believed legal tender legislation would be unconstitutional. Although it periodically debated the merits of such a measure, no proposals were ever accepted.

It is obvious that the Confederate government did not wish to expand its powers to warrant its taking the kind of action the federal government undertook when it made paper notes legal tender. This action by the United States Congress was sustained by the Supreme Court, whose members asserted that since the national existence was threatened by financial instability, a legal tender law was proper. Even though there was no explicit prohibition against such legislation in the Confederate document, the general government could not bring itself to enact a similar statute.

Currency redundancy approached the point where Richmond had to become arbitrary in order to reduce the number of notes outstanding. Under the funding act of October, 1862, all notes issued after December one were to be made fundable in bonds yielding seven per cent interest. The Treasury department was authorized to compel holders of notes issued before such date to fund them in eight per cent bonds within a given time. If these noteholders failed to do so, their notes were made fundable only in seven per cent bonds. This aspect represented a change in the law, because formerly the holders of notes issued before December one had been able to fund their money in eight per cent bonds at any time. In effect the October statute penalized holders who would not fund their notes; still, Memminger maintained that no contract infringement had occurred, declaring that a time limitation on the performance of contracts had never been considered an infringement, where opportunity was "given to claim performance."[13]

In his January, 1863, message to Congress, Davis expressed less optimism about the condition of Confederate finances than he had previously. Referring to the debt, redundancy of currency, inflation and lack of revenue, the President indicated that "energetic and wise legislation" was needed to "prevent serious embarrassment" in monetary affairs. He believed the funding law had been "beneficial," but he realized "it was neither sufficiently prompt or far-reaching to meet the full extent of the evil." [14] One scholar has stated that Richmond's belief that redundancy could be corrected by the absorption of notes into bonds "proved as groundless as similar hopes in the North." [15]

Treasury notes continued to be issued until the total reached more than 600 million dollars in late 1863. By August of the same year 125 millions in notes issued both before and after December one, 1862, had been funded; however, the government's effort at refunding did not proceed with sufficient rapidity. Subsequently, a new note issue was authorized by Congress, and under the law up to 50 million dollars a month could be issued. Richmond's note reduction program was, palpably, unsuccessful, and by January 1, 1864, there were 700 millions in notes outstanding.

All during this time the war was becoming more ominous for the cause, and stimulation of citizen interest in purchasing government bonds was made difficult owing to successive military defeats. Because the central government paid interest on bonds with Treasury notes rather than with specie, the incentive for bond purchases diminished. That the currency situation worsened perceptibly after Vicksburg and Gettysburg was plain, for bonds declined in value and notes again had to be put on the market.

By late 1863 the Confederate financial condition had become grave, and its gravity was reflected in the President's message to Congress: "The state of the public finances is such as to demand your earliest and most earnest attention. I need hardly say that a prompt and efficacious remedy . . . is necessary . . ." [56] Memminger himself conceded the voluntary program of exchanging notes for bonds had not worked, and he acknowledged that statutes had been unable to reduce note circulation to the extent "expected of them." What he appeared to have done was to resign himself to the possibility of having to impose tax penalties on noteholders and to threaten repudiation. When those who opposed such a recourse argued that it would violate the original contract made between the holders of notes and their government, the Secretary would reply that "no contract, however solemn," could "require national ruin." [67]

The Treasury head then proposed that any new note issue be limited and that old notes not funded would cease to be currency after a designated period. A law enacted by Congress in February, 1864, gave noteholders two choices: they could exchange their bills for long-term bonds yielding four per cent interest, or they could exchange them for new notes at the rate of three dollars of the old for two dollars of the new issue. By May the Executive was declaring that the funding act of February had had the "desired effect" and Memminger was asserting that the "financial measures adopted at the last session" had given the "country a new starting point." [18] While the February act had the temporary effect of holding further depreciation in abeyance for a few months, public confidence was reduced by the partial debt repudiation which the act entailed. One scholar has suggested that the unconstitutionality of the law was more definite than that of any possible legal tender statute. In his judgment the former violated a constitutional provision stating that "no law of Congress" could "discharge any debt contracted" before passage of the same. [19]

During the last year currency values were so unstable that the public "would not tie up their credit in rigid bonds." Rather, citizens preferred to use notes in order to make investments in personal property or real estate. As Coulter has emphasized, "people were never sure if or when the government would pay interest on bonds, to say nothing of principal." [20]

George A. Trenholm, Memminger's successor, was more realistic in assessing the currency problem, for he thought the ineffectiveness of funding was traceable to a lack of public confidence in the currency and not just to a redundancy. By the end of the war the amount of notes outstanding had passed the one billion dollar mark — the time had long since passed when the Confederacy could turn back and use a different technique for gaining revenue.

It is not at all comprehensible what measures the government could have taken to finance the war that it did not take. Simply put, the general government did not have enough manpower and economic resources to support a prolonged war which became increasingly modern in its destructiveness. To say that Richmond tried to obtain the financial means to sustain operations within its own sphere of action would be defensible.

2

A more significant facet of the total Confederate financial program concerned its taxing policies. In order to provide revenue for the central government, Congress had the constitutional power to impose duties on goods, and early in 1861 the legislature adopted the contemporary United States tariff laws, which remained in force until altered by subsequent action. What changes Congress did make were intended to broaden the free list to include many articles of necessity, and to impose an export duty of 1/8 of one per cent per pound on all cotton exported in the raw state. In a March amendment a duty of 15 per cent was imposed on specific manufactures of iron and wood. Two months later the legislature enacted a comprehensive tariff; it placed *ad valorem* rates of 5 to 25 per cent on imports, even though Memminger had favored the imposition of a 12½ per cent tax on exports only. Intended to provide revenue for the government, this 1861 tariff law was based on the United States tariffs of 1846 and 1857.

Prematurely, the Treasury head had estimated that import duties would bring in 25 millions during the first year; however, the "blockade dried up hopes" that a tariff would provide any extensive revenues. That Confederate trade declined owing to the Union blockade was apparent, for within months the total exports of cotton dropped from two million to 13,000 bales. In 1860-61 New Orleans exported one and a half million bales of cotton, but the total fell to 11,000 bales in the following year. What this development signified was that revenue gained from import and export duties was going to be negligible.

Confederate leaders had expressed their displeasure over the prewar federal government's fostering of industries through a high protective tariff; yet after the war began, they discouraged foreign trade in order to protect their nascent industry. As one scholar has put it, the "statement of good intentions against a protective tariff did not prevent the development of a strong protectionist sentiment."[21] Davis himself admitted that "injuries resulting from the interruption of foreign commerce" had "received compensation by the development of our internal resources." Only three months after the federal blockade started, an assertion was made that trade restrictions were "a blessing in disguise," the idea being that a blockade would stimulate southern commercial independence.[22]

After having dealt with tariff legislation, Congress turned to its other constitutional powers as outlined in section eight of article one. Granted the power to impose duties to facilitate navigation, the legislature levied a small tonnage tax whose proceeds were to be used to maintain the Confederate lighthouse system. Given the power to regulate foreign and interstate commerce, Congress extended a free transit to goods imported from a foreign country and destined for another. It also gave a duty-free passage to vessels entering the Mississippi river within the Confederacy, provided they were going "to any other point or place beyond" its limits.[23] These legislative actions were taken before the bombardment of Fort Sumter, and were intended to allay concern of the west about shipment of goods down the Mississippi.

The problem of taxation itself was never resolved by the Richmond government. Memminger believed that direct taxes would "pervade the whole body politic," and he urged a program of internal taxation.[24] Congress responded to the Secretary by enacting an August, 1861, bill which placed a direct tax of half of one per cent on specific categories of property within the states of the Confederacy. Under it the tax was apportioned among the states, which were to serve as collecting instruments for the general government.

In his January, 1863, report, Memminger urged the legislature to provide the means to pay the interest and principal on government securities, calling for taxes which would bring in 63 millions per year. Using its power to impose excise taxes, Congress passed a tax law in April, which levied an eight per cent tax on certain agricultural products, a license tax on occupations, a sales tax with rates varying between 2½ and 10 per cent, a tax-in-kind of one tenth of agricultural products raised during the year and a tax on earnings. The latter tax was made payable every January, and it affected salaries and net incomes gained from sources other than salaries. Under the law's provisions an exemption of 1,000 dollars was allowed the taxpayer; if a person's income exceeded this amount, a tax of one per cent was levied on the first 1,500 dollars and two per cent on the excess. While this tax was small, the government did demonstrate by it that as many taxable objects as possible were going to be reached.

Administration of the 1863 law proved an arduous task. Citizens were "confused by the returns called for, and they resented demands made on their incomes," while farmers, unaccustomed to paying such taxes, were antipathetic toward the not easily evaded tax-in-kind.[25] Under the law the tithe was to be taken by the taxpayer to the local post quartermaster depot, where Confederate officials would receive the produce, shipping food commodities directly to the army and cotton to Treasury agents. To expedite the collection of taxes, Richmond set up 338 collection districts in the country; what this development meant was that Confederate citizens would have to pay their taxes directly to officers of the Richmond government. The important consideration here in terms of a federal system is that the state governments were not assigned the job of collecting the money.

In enacting the 1863 tax measure the government had to decide if it could impose direct taxes without apportioning them among the states, for under the permanent Constitution Representatives and direct

taxes had to be apportioned among the states according to their respective numbers. Thus, direct taxes in land and slaves were to be
apportioned among the states on the basis of their free inhabitants
and three-fifths of their slaves. It was intended that a national census
would determine their total numbers; however, since extensive areas
of the Confederacy were lost to the enemy, it proved impracticable
to take a census. Memminger maintained that even if a census were
taken, a tax program based on its findings would fall hard on citizens
living in areas still free of Union troops. Davis, recognizing that direct
taxes could not be levied as prescribed in the Constitution, believed
the only alternative was to make them "uniform through the Confederate States," as outlined in the document for the levying of indirect
or excise taxes.[26] In his opinion the "primary duty" of the Confederate
government was to "execute the general intent" expressed by the fundamental law. Again, the emergency of war compelled the leadership to
give an elastic interpretation to the Constitution.

Early in 1864 Congress approved another tax law, which imposed
a 10 per cent tax on the holdings of gold and silver plate, a 10 per cent
levy on general business profits, a 25 per cent tax on excess profits and
a five per cent tax on all property not otherwise covered by special
taxes. Although this law constituted substantial tax legislation, the
Treasury head claimed the act was "so cumbrous and intricate, that
delay and disappointment" would be "its inevitable results."[27] The
total amount of taxes collected under these two tax laws reached about
120 millions, but this was insufficient for the government's needs.

Public discontent with the laws increased owing to the fact that taxes
were not uniformly collected: this is to say that isolated areas escaped
collection efforts, and the result was that the more accessible territories made the greater contributions. Every year tax collection was
being made more difficult owing to the movement of federal armies,
which were covering more and more ground. By early 1862 the Union
forces in the west had penetrated the Confederacy to the northern
part of Mississippi and had cleared the river as far south as Vicksburg,
federal control extending from New Orleans to Port Hudson, located
just below Vicksburg. By this period Union armies, too, had gained
footholds in the coastal areas of every state except Alabama and Texas;
all of these points served as bases from which federal raids could be
initiated into the interior. That this situation had an adverse effect
on the tax-collecting capacity of the government was evident, because
the territory within which Richmond could collect taxes was becoming
smaller in size.

3

Criticism was directed toward Secretary Memminger for his not having pursued different means to satisfy the government's revenue requirements. General Joseph Johnston, who believed defeat could be traced to the Confederacy's unsteady finances, was critical of the Treasury head for his not having used the 1860-1861 cotton crop to obtain European credits. His contention was that the government should have transported the crop to Europe before the Union blockade became effective .

The difficulty with the Johnston thesis was that Richmond's financial instability was not the cause of defeat; rather it was symptomatic of Confederate inability to achieve independence. Cotton was, moreover, no longer "king" in middle 1861, because, at least for the time being, European stockpiles were adequate. Even though the cotton crop gathered during the 1860-1861 season was estimated at 3,849,000 bales, by early 1861 approximately 600,000 bales were being held by New England textile manufacturers and about three million bales had been shipped abroad.[28] During this period the Treasury Department could not afford to use its limited number of notes to buy cotton in large quantities; furthermore, its Secretary considered it unconstitutional for the government to purchase cotton and thereby assist planters, asserting that no funds belonging to the public should be used for the "relief of any interest." [29] To have carried out the Johnston idea the general government would have required 4,000 vessels to transport cotton to Europe before the beginning of the May, 1861, blockade. These problems led Capers, Memminger's biographer, to suggest that the General's accusation resolved itself "into a fleet of phantom ships loaded with phantom cotton."[30]

Two years later cotton was made the basis for a loan negotiated by Confederate agents in Europe. In this instance government bonds yielded an interest rate of seven per cent to investors, and they were made exchangeable in cotton or redeemable at par. Behind the loan's security was Richmond's pledge that it would deliver the cotton "not later than six months" after peace with the Union.

Early in the war Congress had to concern itself with the disposition of alien property. Under an act of August, 1861, alien property was confiscated; all income derived from the sale of such property was to be used to compensate Confederate citizens who had loss of property claims against the United States government. In accordance with the statute all citizens of the Union had to leave the Confederate States or be regarded as aliens.

The law's constitutionality was sustained by A. G. Magrath, a Confederate district judge in South Carolina, who declared that the government's power to wage war carried with it the authority to confiscate alien property. In arguing Richmond's case before the court, a representative of the Confederate Attorney General's office asserted that confiscation was a sovereign right. His comment was revealing: "Having, then, on this subject, Sovereignty, with all its attributes, the provisional Government stands on the same footing with France, Russia, or Great Britain, in reference to the exercise of the power granted." [31] What he was doing was to acknowledge that in expropriating alien property the general government had sovereignty with all its attributes. Presumably, if the the government had sovereignty or supreme power over sequestration, then the "sovereign" states had no power to deal with the problem. Was sovereignty or supreme political power divided between the states and the "nation" even in the Confederacy? Notice that the representative did not use the term "sovereign power," which Calhoun believed to be only an "attribute" of sovereignty and not sovereignty itself.

Definitive steps were undertaken by Richmond to regulate trade with the enemy and with other foreign countries. Relying on its war power and its power to regulate interstate commerce, Richmond forbade the sale of products such as cotton, tobacco, rice and naval stores in areas under federal occupation. Also forbidden by the government was the shipment of cotton exports through Confederate ports. While some shipments circumvented the blockade, the "Federal fleet prevented any general exportation." [32] By 1863 the central government had reversed Memminger's earlier stand against the use of government money to buy cotton and bought 399,000 bales between April and December, paying the planters in Confederate bonds. A Thomas Bayne was subsequently appointed to give a central supervision to the purchase and export of government cotton, whose proceeds were employed to purchase needed imported goods.

The problem of counterfeiting remained a serious one for the central government throughout the conflict. Constitutionally, the legislature was given the power to provide for restrictions against the practice, and in 1864 it enacted a bill which prohibited persons from dealing in the paper currency of the enemy. Administration of the law proved troublesome, as Confederate money could be readily counterfeited; moreover, it was printed in the north and circulated in the Confederacy in a federal attempt to debase the currency. The law also forbade the circulation of Union money, but Richmond itself made an exception when the government benefited. In order to obtain supplies, the central government would exchange cotton and other commodities for United States greenbacks.

Of continuing seriousness was the problem of inflation which the government appeared unable to arrest. Inflationary pressure was increased because the area over which Richmond could exert control was being compressed all the time. Just consider the situation that obtained in 1864: General Sherman's army was maneuvering into central and eastern Georgia on its approach to Charleston; Richmond was cut off from contacts with states west of the Mississippi; and Grant was laying siege to Petersburg. As the territory over which Confederate authority prevailed became smaller, there occurred a per capita increase in the Treasury notes outstanding: what this development meant was that the price system was being disrupted by the "quantitative infllation" of paper money, Treasury note depreciation and commodity shortages. Goods became scarce as a result of the blockade, enemy raids and the Confederate program of destroying property in danger of federal seizure.

One scholar has suggested that in 1862 the Confederacy was living "through a nightmare of multiple expanding currencies . . . and rocketing prices." [33] The value of the Confederate dollar did not slide below 33 cents until 1863, but two years later it had fallen to only 1.6 cents in gold. A steadily fluctuating price cycle ensued from which there appeared no hope of change for the better, since changing prices encouraged speculative practices by those who wanted something tangible for their money.

The government did attempt to counter inflation, but its actions were too few and too late. It sought to place limitations on the profits of certain businesses, and took the important step of denying military exemption to workers whose employers failed to accept regulations governing profit margins. More specifically, an August, 1863, law forbade the profits of businesses doing government work to exceed 33⅓ per cent; such a restriction applied to profits made on goods sold not only to the military but to civilians as well. During the last two years proposals were introduced in Congress to extend impressment prices to all commercial transactions, but the legislature would not approve any general price-fixing plan.

Proposals were made, too, to regulate speculation; yet none won endorsement from Congress. An 1864 act did levy a ten per cent tax on business profits, its objective being to limit speculative activities; however, this tax represented only a piecemeal attack on the whole problem, since speculation was being fed by the large amounts of paper money being circulated by state governments. Under the 1861 Constitution the central government had the right to coin money and regulate its value, but since it could not constitutionally prevent the states from issuing bills of credit, Richmond could not exert direct controls over the issuance of paper money by them.

President Davis attempted to use his veto power to restrict the issuance of additional Treasury notes, vetoing one measure that authorized the circulation of more notes in order to provide payments for army arrears. In disapproving the bill the Executive asserted that he could not sign it, as the government had made an implicit pledge against further note issues.[34]

Within a federal system it is essential that the central government be enabled to assert its authority directly over individuals through taxation. Obviously, the Confederate tax program affected "national" citizens in a direct way as individuals and not merely as citizens of their respective political communities, the states. Owing to the government's actions people were made aware of the financial powers exercised by Richmond, for it was they who had to pay several kinds of taxes to the general government, including those on income, agricultural land, farm produce, occupations and business profits.

As the war progressed, Richmond's financial needs increased, and a government that once tried to rely on a tariff for its revenue began to impose taxes on business profits. However small these taxes might have been, the point is that the central government did impose them. With the continuation of war the government reached for a wider range of taxable objects to support itself within its own sphere of action. That the extent of its involvement in 1863 differed noticeably from that obtaining two years earlier was clear, for the tax laws made individual citizens conscious of Richmond's constitutional powers. As 1861 gave way to 1865, relationships between the general government and Confederate citizens increased measurably. Circumstances even forced the general government to give up "cherished *laissez faire* ideas," when it initiated a limited profit-fixing program.[35]

All of these actions were taken by a government which, constitutionally, had no sovereignty *per se*. In theory the central government had the "attributes of sovereignty," but sovereignty itself resided only in the states — did it in reality?

VI

CONFEDERATE ADMINISTRATION

The nature of the power structure envisioned for the Confederacy was given a working interpretation in 1861, for it was then that the administration of the general government began to take form. Confronted by the *fait accompli* of secession, Congress initiated actions to establish executive departments whose secretaries would be enabled to implement "national" policy decisions made at Richmond. The administration subsequently organized was capable of exerting direct control over the lives of individual Confederate citizens.

Within a federal system it is important that the central government have the administrative capacity to carry out national laws. While it may be feasible for the government to employ state officials for designated purposes, it should be able to have supervisory control over them, if they are used. In this first year an administrative organization was created by Richmond which facilitated the government's efforts to implement its own objectives within its own sphere of action.

As each state seceded the ownership of United States property was transferred to the state governments; later, seized federal properties were turned over to the Richmond government for its use. The Louisiana convention offered possession of federal lighthouses, mints, customshouses and forts to the Confederacy. In Alabama the convention directed that a marine hospital, revenue cutter and a customhouse be transferred to the control of Richmond, and it instructed the collector of customs to relinquish all collected money to the Confederacy.

Continuity for administrative operations was ensured, because each state passed ordinances providing that federal officials and laws pertaining to them should remain unaffected by secession. To illustrate: the Louisiana convention permitted land office registrars and receivers to remain at their positions, although they had to take a new oath and execute new bonds in the name of the state.

More generally, the provisional Congress at Montgomery sought to make easy the transition of government to the Confederacy by declaring that all United States laws in force within the Confederate States on November 1, 1860, and not in conflict with the 1861 Constitution, should remain in effect until repealed. In more detailed terms a Congressional law provided, for example, that officers holding customs jobs when the Confederate Constitution went into effect should be appointed to the same offices.

As early as February, 1861, Congress began to provide for the establishment of the executive departments. Both the Treasury and War departments were organized late in the month, and in close succession the other departments were constituted. Under the acts providing for their establishment the responsibilities of each major officeholder were specifically detailed by Congress. The Secretary of War was, for example, directed to take charge of all matters pertaining to the army, the Indian tribes and such other duties as the President might assign him.[1]

There was created a Postoffice department, whose postmasters and special agents were to continue performing their tasks in "strict conformity with such existing laws" that were not in conflict with Confederate laws or with the Constitution.[2] John Reagan, the Postmaster General, indicated in May, 1861, that the government would take over the federal postal system by June 1. Continuous operation was assured, because contracts which had already been made by United States officials were continued in effect. Obtaining personnel who had held key positions in the federal service, the Postmaster General "practically transferred the brains" of the Washington department to the Confederate.[3] By late 1861 there were 8,411 postmasters in the service, and 2,500 persons were under contract to carry mail for the government.

The organizational requirements of the Navy department were met by bureaus of orders and details, ordnance and hydrography, provisions and clothing, and medicine and surgery. Additionally, there was created a policy-making board, consisting of the Secretary and two aides, which was intended to pass on general naval strategy and issue instructions to the departmental administration. Opportunely for the Confederacy, about one fifth of United States naval officers resigned from service to enter the Confederate.

Bureaus were similarly organized to operate the Attorney General's office, the War and Treasury departments. A bureau of public printing, assistant Attorney General, a patent office and the Attorney General's office itself constituted the legal department. As for the patent office, the expectation was that it would become self-sustaining financially. Within the War department the quartermaster, commissary, ordnance, medical, niter and mining, and engineer bureaus were created. Although the department employed thousands of persons in

Richmond and elsewhere, the State department had few personnel needs owing to the failure of the Confederacy to win foreign recognition. Within the Treasury department were the office of the commissioner of taxes, a produce loan office, a treasury note division and a cotton tax bureau. Again, federal personnel who had resigned from the United States government filled most of the departmental positions.

That all of these departments had an organizational structure patterned on that of their federal counterparts was apparent. One scholar has pointed out that the quartermaster bureau was a "photographical reproduction of the old United States organization."[4] As for the Treasury department, Memminger used the "cumbersome but effective organization" of Alexander Hamilton.[5] Because both federal personnel and organizational patterns were used, this condition had an effect on the administrative process, for it meant that an administrative establishment structured after the federal model would nurture the development of "national" powers and responsibilities. Comprehensibly, former officeholders of the Washington government would be influenced by their prewar administrative experiences.

Care was exercised by Congress in delineating the purposes for which public monies were appropriated, and the object type of classification arrangement was used. Under an 1862 act funds were, illustratively, granted for salaries of the Secretary of War, the assistant secretary and other officials, a total of 80,000 dollars being appropriated explicitly for the object of paying their salaries. At the same time the ordnance bureau was given 11 million dollars.[6] A later statute gave the department one million dollars to buy pig and rolled iron, and granted it 500,000 dollars to purchase casting cannon, shot and shells. The relevance here is that in each instance the object of the appropriation was expressly stated in the law.

Under Confederate law the expenditure requirements of the departments were to be collected by the Secretary of the Treasury, who then was to give them to Davis prior to a new meeting of Congress. In practice the Secretary compiled the estimates and forwarded them to the legislature with his recommendations; what the development substantiated was that the Treasury department would retain control over the expenditure of funds by the other departments and would serve as a depository from which each department would have to draw funds for its expenditures.

Confederate personnel policies were followed in accordance with the Constitution. While the assistant secretaries and bureau chiefs had to be nominated by the President and confirmed by the Senate, they were not independent of the department heads, as they could be relieved for cause or suspended at the pleasure of the secretaries, provided the latter had obtained the approval of Davis. Those farther down the administrative hierarchy were subject to the supervisory control of the department secretaries. The Treasury head was given the authority, for example, to appoint a chief clerk and such other clerks as he might consider necessary and Congress might authorize. He could distribute clerks among the bureaus, and could move them in a way that would "best subscribe the public interest." [7]

Palpably, then, Richmond had the organization to administer Confederate laws and undertake activities on its own. If the general government within a federal system is to function effectively in its sphere of action, it needs a reasonably complete administration. As a general rule, the central government's activities were undertaken by departmental officials who operated within the several states. Importantly, these officials were not required to act through the instrumentality of the state governments, and the actions taken by them were not made dependent on any sanction given them by the states.

2

Lacking an industrial base to support a prolonged conflict, the government had to promote economic ventures on its own. To establish itself as a separate nation, the Confederacy had to initiate programs to build an economy to sustain a war effort. Manifestly, the idea of the government's granting money to private business was contrary to the states' rights philosophy expressed in the 1861 Constitution; yet the war forced the general government to alter the framers' view of its limited purposes. It was one matter to show political disdain for governmental stimulation of industry, but it was another to prosecute a war without being assured of minimal material requirements. Within Congress there was a vocal states' rights element which opposed the assumption of centralizing activities by Richmond, and it would be unrealistic to minimize its influence, but the majority realized the government had to participate in a variety of economic undertakings.

Prodded by demands for niter, Congress made money advances to private manufacturers of the product; owners who developed new mines were given a legislative inducement amounting to 50 per cent of the equipment cost. But Congress soon went beyond inducement alone, and began to offer to meet one-half of the costs required to establish businesses with which the government had made contracts.

It authorized Davis to "advance a third of the value" of contemplated output in iron and coal for stockpiling purposes.

Confederate involvement in the economy was not limited to the legislature's granting financial aid. To develop "all the mineral resources of the Confederacy," a nitre and mining corps was organized in 1862; within three months after its beginning the bureau was operating 16 nitre caves and employing about 400 workers.[8] By July the bureau had "refined 60,000 pounds of nitre, taken over and enlarged two lead mines, and erected an admirable smelting work at Petersburg."[9] New responsibilities were added to the bureau's work load, and it began to oversee the production of iron, copper, lead and minerals. An 1864 report indicated it was engaged in rebuilding destroyed furnaces and in producing iron supplies.

Government control was similarly exerted over the salt industry. The subsistence bureau of the War department early operated salt works, an army general supervising salt mining in New Iberia, Louisiana. By the third year of the war the bureau was operating works which covered three-quarters of a square mile at Saint Andrew's Bay on the Florida coast.

Government involvement in the economy also extended to the building of armories, foundries, shops and powder mills by the quartermaster and ordnance bureaus of the War department. Particularly effective work was done by Josiah Gorgas in the ordnance bureau: "We began . . . without an arsenal, laboratory or powder mill of any capacity . . . and before the close of 1863 . . . we had built . . . almost literally out of the ground foundries . . . and a chain of arsenals . . . equal in their capacity . . . to the best of those in the United States"[10]

The Navy department operated powder plants at Columbia, South Carolina, and Augusta, Georgia, and a rope works at Petersburg, Virginia. During the first two years the department made 30 contracts for the building of 40 vessels; a year later the department had established machine shops, five ordnance workshops and 18 shipyards. By the end of the war the Navy was operating a grist mill at Albany, Georgia, several rolling mills, iron furnaces and niter works. To repair cannons, swords and guns, the War department established an arsenal at Atlanta, which served as the main entrepot for the quartermaster and commissary bureaus of the department. A government arsenal at Augusta early reported that means would be found to "complete manufacture of everything connected with artillery but the guns themselves."[11]

Not having enough clothing for the military, the Confederacy estalished quartermaster depots under military auspices, and operated garment shops at Augusta, Atlanta and Columbus, Georgia, shoe shops being located in the latter two cities. At one period the job of manufacturing shoes for the military was monopolized by government-supervised shops; the reason was that since Richmond controlled the distribution of hides and leather, it could assert a direct influence over these shops. One shoe and saddle factory operated by the government in Richmond had a shoe-making capacity of 1,000 pairs per day.

These were not the only involvements of the general government. Because it could not secure adequate medicinal supplies, the Confederate surgeon general supervised the establishment of medical laboratories at Charlotte, Columbia, Macon and Lincolnton. To secure needed arms, the chief ordnance officer of the army found it essential to take over the Cranberry Iron Works and the Salisburg machine shop in North Carolina. That these various bureaus became "small manufacturing empires" was necessary, for Richmond's munition, food, medical and clothing requirements had to be fulfilled.

Financial stimulus was used by the government to encourage construction of railroad lines and telegraph facilities, both of which were essential to the prosecution of the war. In 1863 the President was authorized by Congress to make contracts for a road connecting the Richmond & Danville and North Carolina lines. The legislature also gave its authorization to an extension of a $150,000 loan to the Alabama and Mississippi Company to build a line between Selma and Meridian, which was completed near the end of 1862.[12] To promote the construction of a line between Rome, Georgia, and Blue Mountain, Alabama, Congress appropriated more than one million dollars, although the road was not ready before the war's close. It has been estimated that the Confederacy subsidized the construction of about 200 miles of railroad lines. In addition, the government granted a subsidy of 8,000 dollars to build a telegraph line between Little Rock and Fort Smith.

Constitutionally, the legislature was forbidden to use any provision in the document to justify its appropriating money for internal improvements that would facilitate commerce. A general welfare clause was omitted from the Constitution to obviate an elastic interpretation of Congressional powers; yet to warrant the government's taking the kinds of actions it did, a latitudinous interpretation had of necessity to be given the document. Even in the Confederacy the necessary and proper clause could be used to give an expansion to specific powers, such as those to declare war, raise armies and maintain a navy. Since there was nothing in the Constitution that justified some of its activities, the government had to assume it had the implied power to act, but this was the development to which southerners had indicated their opposition under the Washington experience.

The urgencies of war did not allow the general government to maintain a *laissez faire* attitude toward the economy. As Charles Ramsdell has pointed out, "all theoretical considerations" against government intervention in the private sector of the economy deferred to wartime needs.[13] It was through its command of labor, which the legislature provided for in an 1862 act, that Richmond was enabled to fill its supply requirements, for under the law Congress authorized the exemption of workers essential to industry, employees in cotton, woolen and paper mills being included among the many categories of exemptees. A determination about whether or not the affected employees should gain exemption from military service was given to the Secretary of War.

To inhibit excessive profits from being made by businesses having government contracts, the War department provided that company employees would gain exemption if profits remained below 75 per cent of production costs, the limitation applying to goods sold to both the army and civilians. Later in the conflict the department sought to limit profits to about one-third of the cost of production; what the government was seeking to do was to demonstrate its willingness to use the conscript power to curb the making of markedly high returns on government contracts.

The extent of government controls increased during the 1863 period, and manufacturers began to find it more difficult to convince enrolling officers that their employees were necessary to production. When the labor supply declined, factories "rarely dared" to refuse making a contract with one of the government agencies; usually, a government threat to revoke their labor exemptions was "enough to bring them to terms."[14] A later act of 1864 gave the local enrolling officers considerable discretion in honoring or declining requests for labor exemptions, which were limited to two months, although they could be renewed.

During the last two years of the war Richmond made it a policy to require cotton and woolen factories to set aside a major part of their output for the Confederate military. If a manufacturer proved obdurate, the government would use its exemption authority to encourage compliance. Since the central government also established a system of priorities on the railroads, a manufacturer could not easily decline military requests for goods, and the fact that the army quartermaster general could prevent the shipment of raw materials to a producer served to prod him into acceding to the government's wishes. As early as 1863 Virginia factories were being brought under the administrative control of the quartermaster general; in later months factories in the lower south discovered they too had to accommodate themselves to the government's requests if they wanted to remain in operation. Even during the second year of war Richmond had obtained a monopoly on raw wool supplies, and by having a monopoly the government could compel factories to produce entirely on its own account.

Because bureau chiefs in the War department could decide which manufacturers should gain exemption for employees, they held influential positions concerning contract negotiations. As Vandiver has said: "In this power lay a coercive potential strong enough to command cooperation from almost all private industrialists who wished to stay in operation." He concludes: "By 1863 control exercised by the Confederate government over private industries had already grown to such proportions as to dictate completely the activities of such plants . . ." [15] Still, the government found the exercise of control over North Carolina factories to be troublesome, as owners there were supported politically by their states' rights governor, Zebulon Vance.

Industrial workers were not alone in gaining exemption from service, as agricultural workers were also included in the exemption program. Florida farmers could win exemption by agreeing to produce certain commodities for the War department's commissary bureau, but if the farmer violated his contract with the government, he was then made subject to the draft and loss of his bond.

By imposing restrictions on railroad operations, Congress revealed it was willing to exert control over the country's transporation system. Although the Executive was disinclined to use completely the authority given him under Congressional law, a system of priorities was set up by the War department to facilitate the transporation of war supplies. Again, according to Vandiver: "After the Quartermaster General had instituted a system of . . . priorities . . . the railroads were unable to carry anything not specifically contributing to the war effort." [16] Admittedly, the attempt to establish a workable system of freight car exchange and to set up rates for private business was unsuccessful but the government did succeed in giving public freight a first priority over private. Those trains operating between the blockade-running port of Wilmington and elsewhere had to carry one-half of their capacity in government freight. That not all problems affecting the railroads were administrative in nature was evident, for operations were hampered by federal forays and by the lack of sufficient iron.

Two months before the end of the war the Secretary of War was authorized by Congress to "assume control of any road needed for military purposes." At this juncture the military situation was becoming urgent, and the legislature was prepared to forego its states' rights scruples and allow the exertion of more intensive controls over the roads. Despite the deficiencies in operation, the railroads were instrumental in furthering the cause: "Poorly as the railroads were run, partly through mismanagement and partly from the impossibility of obtaining materials to maintain them in order, they contributed largely to keep the Southern cause going." [17]

Telegraph operations as well were made subject to centralized control. Initially, the nominal control of all lines was taken over by the Confederate Postmaster General, and a civilian, William S. Morris, President of the Confederate Telegraph Company, became chief of military telegraph. That he succeeded in his task was attested to by a historian of the Confederate telegraph: the maintenance of an "effective telegraph system through the South . . . won for him the wholehearted praise of Reagan." [18] For his part, Postmaster General Reagan would not intervene in private management of the lines, unless military requirements made it mandatory, but the point is that this power was available for use by Richmond. One scholar has remarked: "Knowledge of this power, if nothing else, generally made more than nominal control unnecessary." [19]

Since private companies succeeded in meeting military telegraph necessities, the army telegraph organization existed only in scattered local areas. What did occur occasionally was that the local military commander would take charge of lines if necessary. In one situation General Pierre G. T. Beauregard detailed operators from the ranks and used them in the Charleston, South Carolina, area to maintain communications. In any case, the Confederate telegraph system proved itself: "Codes unknown to the supervisory agents at the principal points and news accounts detailing troop movements, the positions of particular units or their strength were denied transmission." [20]

The government's attention was turned, too, in the direction of controls over trade with the enemy. Legislative regulation proved to be arduous owing to the fact that it was not only private traders who engaged in clandestine operations, but the Confederacy's produce loan bureau itself became a participant in "all sorts of devious operations." [21] Richmond acquired large quantities of cotton which were then bartered for needed goods, and after Vicksburg contracts were negotiated by the government to dispense its cotton through Union lines. Wanting to reduce abusive practices, the general government did station an agent at Jackson, Mississippi, "to whom both state and Confederate cotton were to be entrusted for exchange." [22]

All of these multi-faceted activities of the central government were sustainable by the supremacy clause of the 1861 Constitution, and when the government used the powers given it, actions taken to carry out these powers had to be given a superior constitutional status.

3

It was in the implementation of government programs that Richmond made its impression on the individual citizen. Using its own personnel or supervising state officials when they assisted in carrying out Richmond's programs, the general government asserted its authority directly over the people as a whole. In a brief time sequence of four years the administrative influence of the government became all-pervasive. To illustrate: even at the county level of government, boards of investigation, established to pass on applications for exemptions from service, were subject to War department supervision.

Under the conscript law responsibility for enrolling Confederate draftees was given the President and his Secretary of War, who proceeded to issue instructions pertaining to the enrollment, training and use of conscripts. Camps of instruction were established in every state; at their head were military commanders who supervised the administrative activities of enrolling officers located within the Confederate states. To assist the government in evaluating the conscript program, commanders would convene their enrolling officers in order to have monthly meetings, which were ordered midway in the war by Colonel John S. Preston, chief of the Confederate conscript bureau. Inspectors were, moreover, sent out by the bureau in Richmond to remove ineffectual enrolling officers and to "set aside improper decisions" made by them. [23]

Although men were not conscripted into the Confederate army through the instrumentality of the state governments, Davis could use state officers in enrolling conscripts, provided he had the approval of the governors concerned. In the event the relationship proved unworkable, the President was authorized under the law to use Confederate personnel exclusively. Whoever was used, the point is that the official was subject to War department regulations, and in implementing the conscription laws the enrolling officers had to follow the department's instructions. Significantly, the War department served as a review authority in hearing cases appealed to it from enrolling officials.

At the outset several governors anticipated they would be able to influence the administration of conscription; however, their expectations were soon disillusioned by the government. In 1862 Governor John G. Shorter of Alabama questioned the wisdom of calling on state officers to implement a law which had been "discharged and directed solely" by Richmond officials. Yet his attitude was not commonly shared: "Governors yielded generally with good grace and allowed such militia officers as they had . . . to be used by Confederate authorities."

Administrative difficulties in implementing conscription were compounded when both the army and the conscript bureau tried competitively to enroll men. In the Trans-Mississippi region conscription was carried out by military commanders who reported to the Secretary of War, but east of the river the program was to be administered by the bureau, located in the adjutant and inspector general's office in Richmond. Competition between the eastern army and the bureau began in 1863, when General Braxton Bragg, the area military commander, authorized General Gideon J. Pillow to organize a "volunteer and conscript recruiting bureau" with headquarters at Huntsville, Alabama. Pillow's officers were sent to areas within the state and to neighboring Mississippi and Tennessee, and the conflict developed when Bragg declined to recognize the conscript bureau's "exclusive control over the whole subject of conscription." [24] For a period of several months the Richmond bureau discovered itself supervising the program in the seaboard states, while its military counterpart implemented conscription in Florida, Tennessee, Alabama and Mississippi. The impasse continued during the middle part of 1863, and its consequence was to debilitate the program's implementation.

As far as Preston was concerned, the substitution of the military for bureau services provided not a remedy but "an additional drawback." [25] His belief was that the law would be administered more efficiently if responsibility were given the bureau alone. Throughout this period of administrative bifurcation Preston was kept appraised of the General's activities by bureau field inspectors who dispatched reports to Richmond. Eventually, the conscript bureau regained complete responsibility for carrying out the program.

Later, administrative conflict evolved between the conscript bureau chief and the generals of reserves, which were composed of conscripts ordered into Confederate service to defend their home states. Under the law their commanders were to implement conscription "under the the direction of the Secretary of War, through the Conscript Bureau." [26] But one commander, General James L. Kemper in Virginia, was reluctant to accept the bureau as part of the chain of command, asserting that the bureau served only as a channel of communication by which he could get in touch with the Secretary of War. In this situation the administrative process was threatened by sterilization for the time being.

It is clear that the over-all performance of the conscript bureau was positive; the final report issued in 1865 indicated that 177,000 men had been conscripted from areas east of the Mississippi. It is not, however, known how many draft eligibles volunteered on account of the program's existence, and the result is that an evaluation of the bureau's activities cannot be made.

Administratively, a perplexing problem for the government was concerned with the impressment of property required by the military. Initially, army purchasing agents would impress supplies, even if their owners declined to sell them at the prices offered. In Mississippi Confederate officials "roamed the state seizing slaves, horses, food, and even houses." [27] Confronted by emergencies, Confederate officials "fell into the habit of taking what they wanted and paying less than the prevailing price." [28] Although impressment was given a formal statutory sanction under the 1863 law, abuses persisted as impressment continued. Coulter has pointed out that many were the "ubiquitous activities of the pressmen" who made raids on property, and took wagons and "anything else" they wanted. [29]

At the operating level impressment was carried out by commissary and quartermaster officers of the War department, whose task was to "furnish any supplies or other property necessary for the army." [30] Agents of the Commissary General, Lucian B. Northrop, operated in the states and were held directly responsible to him. Unfortunately for the public image of the bureau, it never had sufficient funds with which to pay for impressed supplies. What irritated citizens was that quartermasters would take supplies before leaving a final account of their impressment; later on, these same citizens were often unable to obtain compensation for impressed supplies, since they lacked any proof of seizure. In order to receive claims for impressed commodities and forage, claims agents of the government were located in every Congressional district.

The impressment law had not been in effect long before it began to agitate several governors. At one time Henry W. Allen of Louisiana complained that Confederate officers had taken property in a "peremptory and insolent" manner, "simply leaving their receipts for the same." [31] Mississippi's chief executive criticized the government for its having "impressed everything within its reach." [32] That the government did succeed in impressing provisions in North Carolina was attested to by a remark of its states' rights-conscious governor, Zebulon Vance, who said in 1863: "I allude to illegal seizures of property and other depredations of an outrageous character by detached bands of troops — chiefly cavalry." [33] Long hostile to Richmond, the governor acknowledged that the "country was swarming with agents of the Confederate government, stripping bare our markets." [34] With a worsening of the military situation, "wandering companies" of Confederate cavalry began to "live off the country in free-booting fashion." [35]

Confederate officials did not stop with the impressment of provisions alone, for they also seized iron for use on the railroads. In 1862 the military superintendent of the Selma-Meridian project impressed 28 miles of rail beloning to the Alabama and Florida railroad. Confederate seizure of railroad iron and equipment troubled Governor Joseph Brown of Georgia, who complained to the Ordnance Chief in Richmond: "Unless the Confederate authorities cease to impress rolling stock of the State Road, I shall be obligated to stop entirely the transportation of coal over the road." [36] Still, government agents continued to impress and redistribute rolling stock and rails, and when iron could not be bought at a fair price, it was "seized at the specific price determined by the Inspector General's office in Richmond." [37]

It was not only the War department that impressed railroad equipment; the Navy also impressed spare rails which were used to cover ironclads or Confederate gunboats. Because the railroads discovered their equipment could be impressed and their employees conscripted, they had to comply with government demands. One scholar has contended that the roads fell "more and more under the control of the War Department which forced them to do its bidding." [38]

Understandably, the extent to which Richmond used state personnel in implementing Confederate laws varied from place to place and from time to time. After taking charge of the conscript bureau, Colonel Preston ordered completion of the bureau's staff "according to law" which provided for the replacement of state officers by Confederate officials, when necessary. While willing to accept assistance from the state officials, Preston declined to "substitute them for the proper officers prescribed." [39] In order to implement the direct tax measure of 1861, Richmond generally used the tax-collecting agencies of state governments; however, since the chief collectors in each were appointed by the President, the general government retained supervisory control over them. Only in Texas and Mississippi did Confederate personnel directly collect the tax. In carrying out the tax act of two years later the Treasury department took upon itself the task of appraising all property for tax purposes and collecting the taxes. Collection of the tax-in-kind was made by agents acting under War department supervision, and the tithe tax was collected by more than 60 Confederate officials under a Colonel Larkin Smith. Later, collection of the tobacco tithe was administered by the Treasury department.

Implementation of the tax laws created administrative complexities for Richmond. To decentralize Treasury operations and to expedite the government's financial business, assistant Confederate treasurers were located at Mobile and Columbia. Since large disbursements were made, and numerous Treasury notes issued and deposited, such Treasury department suboffices took on increasing importance. At one point Secretary Memminger observed that those at Richmond, Montgomery, Jackson and Charleston had become influential banking institutions. Still, the Confederate tax commissioner once lamented that innumerable obstacles confronted the department as it attempted to administer the laws, asserting that these obstacles could be seen by "any one" who would "inspect the mass of paper required for each return" and the questions asked of taxpayers. [40]

Many, too, were the administrative problems encountered by the Post Office department as it began operations. The most serious one centered on the department's need to cover an area of 700,000 square miles through the means of an inadequate rail system. Under the Constitution the department was supposed to be self-supporting, and Reagan succeeded in making a profit, but he did so by vacating small stations, reducing the franking privileges of members of Congress, charging high rates and bargaining advantageously with railroads to haul the mail. In spite of accumulated difficulties the "post office did manage to handle the mails." [41]

It would be inaccurate to say that implementation of the government's policies was devoid of administrative deficiencies; nevertheless, the general accomplishments were encouraging from the standpoint of Richmond's interests. That an administrative organization was created at all, was no small achievement, for it substantiated the idea that the central government could retain control over its own operations. By employing its own personnel and supervising state officials when used, Richmond was enabled to operate more or less autonomously within the sphere of action given it in the Constitution. Criticism of Confederate adminstration needs to be modified in the realization that there existed a hiatus between the states' rights bias of 1861 and the embodiment of states' rights beliefs in purposive actions by the government.

VII

THE SOUTHERN JUDICIARY

Within a governmental system the judiciary is least susceptible to changes that are made with abruptness in society; what is a commonly experienced condition was of even more applicability in 1861, when few changes were effected in the judiciary as the functions of government were taken over by the Confederacy. To assume that substantial changes would have emanated from secession would be mistaken, for southerners had revered the 1787 Constitution in so far as they interpreted its meaning. President Davis conceded the United States document "was the model followed throughout, with only such changes as experience suggested for better practical working or for greater perspicuity." [1]

Between secession and the formation of a provisional government in Richmond each state enacted measures providing for the transfer of judicial business. The South Carolina convention vested the authority of the late federal judiciary in its own courts. Admiralty and maritime jurisdiction was conferred on the circuit courts for the district of Charleston; furthermore, the state's highest court was granted the power to exercise jurisdiction given formerly to the United States Supreme Court. [2]

These actions were repeated by other states as they withdrew from the Washington government. In Florida the convention inaugurated a system of circuit courts; thereafter, all cases considered by the recent federal courts were to be submitted to the new courts. The records of the various divisions of the late federal district court in the northern part of the state were given to the circuit courts, which were to convene now in St. Augustine, Apalachicola, Pensacola and Tallahassee. The court clerk in each was given duties performed recently by United States commissioners. In Louisiana the convention provided that United States laws relating to the jurisdiction and organization of circuit and district courts were to be honored, and henceforth all suits pending in the state were to be prosecuted in its name. Besides, the convention re-enacted and recognized formally the criminal laws of the United States; in the future prosecution for violation of the latter's criminal codes was to be accomplished under state authority.

To replace the circuit and district courts of the United States, the Georgia convention established two new jurisdictions, which were designated as the northern and southern district courts of the "Independent State of Georgia." The Alabama convention passed ordinances transferring jurisdiction of the federal courts to circuit and chancery courts; jurisdiction over admiralty cases was given to the circuit courts and to the municipal court of Mobile. These courts, together with the chancery courts, were now to try cases arising formerly within the jurisdiction of federal courts. Original and exclusive jurisdiction over cases affecting ambassadors and other public ministers was granted to the supreme court. Circuit court clerks were given custody of all records left by the Washington government, and procedural forms used previously by the federal courts were copied for use by the new courts. In cases appealed to the United States Supreme Court from the Alabama high court, the latter was to render decisions as though no appeal had been made; moreover, it was authorized by the convention to adjudicate cases which came on appeal from federal district courts.

Thus, in one action after another the judicial business of United States courts was transferred to state courts, to which jurisdiction was assigned only until the establishment of the Confederate court system. Since the time between secession and formation of the central government was brief, one scholar has contended that these actions were of "little practical effect"; [3] still, these courts took upon themselves new jurisdiction and enlarged authority during the interregnum.

Through early 1861 care was taken to ensure a facile transfer of laws from the Washington government to the Confederate. Under a February act of Congress, all United States laws in force within the Confederate States on November 1, 1860, and not in conflict with the new Constitution were to remain in effect. All of these laws were to be valid until Congress altered or repealed them; what this development alluded to was the conservative nature of the withdrawal from the Union. Under Confederate law the Attorney General of the Confederacy was to give opinions on questions of law whenever requested to do so by the President or any cabinet member; further, he was required to prosecute suits before the to-be-organized Supreme Court whenever the general government was a participant.

In addition, Congress provided that each state was now to serve as the territorial limits for Confederate district court jurisdiction, whose courts were given jurisdiction concurrent with state courts to adjudicate specific civil suits, where a definite monetary value was involved and where the character of the parties warranted review.

State laws were to be considered as rules of judgment by Confederate courts wherever applicable; an exception to this general rule was to obtain where the "constitution, treaties or statutes of the Confederate States" might otherwise require. United States laws pertaining to crimes and offenses, and the procedural methods used in these cases, were to form the rules of practice in Confederate district courts, which were, however, to follow proceedings that were consistent with the Constitution and laws of the Confederacy. Admiralty proceedings in effect under admiralty courts of the United States on December 20, 1860, were continued in "full force" under Confederate courts. All the records, depositions and proceedings relative to any existing suit in the United States circuit or district courts were transferred to the Confederate courts, and wherever there was a judgment of the United States Supreme Court that remained unexecuted in cases appealed from a district court, the Confederate courts had to execute them. These court actions were to be carried out "as if there had been no dissolution" of the Union, provided the judgments had been handed down before secession.[4]

According to Congressional law, the Confederate district courts were given "original cognizance . . . of all actions . . . arising" under the copyright and patent laws of the Confederate States. Their jurisdiction extended to admiralty, maritime and prize cases, naturalization, crimes and offenses recognized under the Confederacy, seizures and forfeitures under the revenue and navigation laws, and the laws of nations.[5] Where a controversy involved subjects other than those indicated in the Confederate treaties or laws, district court jurisdiction was to be limited to cases at suit where $5,000 or more was involved.

Confederate court jurisdiction was restricted to parties listed in the Constitution: this is to say, citizens claiming land under the grants of different states; a citizen and foreign states, their subjects or citizens; a state as plaintiff against citizens of another state or against a foreign state. Under the permanent Constitution all diversity of citizenship cases were removed from Confederate court jurisdiction, the result being that courts of the general government would not consider controversies between citizens of different states. That these states' righters did not want to have a common arbiter decide cases affecting citizens of the "sovereign" states was evident.

Understandably, efficient operation of the Confederate district courts was hindered by the movement of Union armies toward the interior after Vicksburg and Gettysburg. Yet, these courts handed down decisions on constitutional disputes, authorized the sequestration of properties belonging to enemy aliens, condemned prizes and heard a wide range of cases at common law, in admiralty and equity. Through the making of these decisions the district courts extended judicial support to the central government when it operated within its own sphere of action.

As the Confederate courts were being organized, they inherited civil and criminal dockets of United States courts. No person under arrest was released, and all warrants issued by the federal courts were returned to the new courts. Indictments returned by federal grand juries were turned over to Confederate petite juries; persons convicted of having committed offenses against the federal government were imprisoned at Confederate expense.

Since a majority of the federal judges who had renounced their allegiance to the Washington government were reappointed to serve on the Confederate courts, it is not unusual that the new judiciary adhered to the principle of *stare decisis,* under which previous decisions were allowed to stand. As a consequence, cases initiated before the new courts were decided on the basis of judgments rendered formerly under United States court precedents. One scholar has concluded that the Confederate judiciary recognized the applicability of prewar decisions "with as much grace . . . as if there had been no change" in government.

As early as March, 1861, Congress authorized the establishment of a Confederate Supreme Court; but a later measure suspended the convening of any court until it could be organized under the permanent Constitution, and this action was as far as the court issue ever went. President Davis foresaw the desirability of creating a court, and in February had referred to the government's obligation to organize one. At this early period the Attorney General, Thomas Bragg, suggested, too optimistically, that the court would "doubtless be organized in a short time." [6] Even though successive Attorneys General urged Congress to create a court, their pleas proved to be of no avail. By 1863 the incumbent Attorney General was writing to the Executive: "The many conflicting decisions, under the confiscation, conscription, and other laws . . . show, but too plainly, the necessity for prompt action on the part of Congress." [7] A Mississippian expressed the principal reason for the lack of a high court when he said that Confederate leaders "were too busy with the war." [8]

Present generally in the legislature was a commonly held belief that establishment of a supreme court would favor Richmond; having objected to the centralist decisions of the federal court, these leaders did not wish to risk another. As Moore has pointed out: "When the great powers of the Confederate Government were unsheathed by the courts, the new government looked so much like the old one that it was painful to the ultra States' rights men." [9] Southerners, fearing they might set up a judicial catalyst with a centralist influence, decided to "steer clear of pitfalls" in dealing with the court issue.

Opponents of the court in the Confederate Senate included Wigfall, who argued that Justice Marshall's inclination to favor the Washington government had contributed to a dissolution of the 1787 Union. For their parts, William Yancey and Edward Pollard were disturbed by the possibility that a common arbiter would be positioned above the sovereign states. In Curry's opinion a court should not be allowed to change "every power inhering in the State governments, or undelegated by the people, so as to exempt its own action from their influence," while Senator Oldham felt the doctrines set forth in Congressional debate over the court issue would "have well become the rankest Federalists." [10] Some members of Congress did not want to give Davis even more appointing power than he already had; moreever, they did not appreciate the persuasive influence that Judah Benjamin was having on the Executive. As politicians, they realized Benjamin's influence would have predominance in the selection of court appointees.

Yet the proposed court had its supporters among members of Congress. Senator Hill of Georgia early asserted that it was "high time the judicial department be thoroughly organized." His opinion was that the question had been a "lingering concern long enough"; [11] by 1863 Hill thought the creation of a court was a "present necessity." [12] In debating the question he alluded to the fact that numerous appeals from Confederate district courts were awaiting judgment from a high court. Despite this and other expressions of support, the legislature as a whole remained adamant against establishing a court; even though bills providing for its creation were submitted periodically to the Congress, they never won approval.

It is accurate to say that some constitutional questions were left unsettled owing to the absence of a supreme court, but this circumstance was not deleterious to Confederate interests. For Richmond's actions were sustained by favorable decisions of the Confederate district courts, opinions of the Attorneys General and the state supreme courts.

In order to secure a legal opinion concerning the government's use of its powers, Davis would turn to his Attorney General. Successive legal officers were asked to decide questions relating to terms of military service, illegal impressment, and pay and allowances. They considered questions pertaining to the organization of special troops, the authority to appoint military officers and the jurisdiction of military courts. Furthermore, Davis turned to the legal officer for advice on how to deal with recalcitrant governors.

As might be expected, the large majority of the 218 opinions delivered by the Attorneys General was requested by the War, Navy and Treasury departments. Although military questions predominated, the legal officers had to reach opinions concerning Treasury operations as well. The legal department was called on to interpret refunding acts which were passed by Congress to prevent inflation. Fundamentally, the problem before the Attorney General in each case was that of determining the "intent of Congress" in enacting this kind of legislation.

Although the initial Attorneys General gave opinions that questioned the validity of state laws, the later officers declined to co-opt a judicial review power all their own. Both Wade Keyes and George Davis maintained that if the Executive wanted a particular state law invalidated, he should request action from the governor and legislature; further, they believed they had no right to hold acts of Congress to be in violation of the Constitution. George Davis saw his duty to be one of advising the President against approving a measure that appeared to violate the fundamental law; he contended that after the Executive had approved a bill, he, as Attorney General, could not presume the right to declare the law invalid.[13]

Serving as the government's legal officer in 1862, Thomas Watts had to reach decisions on controversies involving conscription. In one opinion he reversed an earlier one by Benjamin, who had held that there were two bodies of troops in the Confederate army, the Confederate and state. Because there were two bodies, Benjamin concluded that the governors could make appointments or fill vacancies in the state ranks. But Watts' opinion was that all men taken into Confederate service were subject to direction by the President. The making of this distinction was important because it meant the general government could retain control over its own military program.

Another opinion delivered by Watts concerned the power of Congress to raise armies. In a May, 1862, opinion the Attorney General held that the Constitution gave the legislature the discretion to decide on "any mode" of raising and supporting the army of the central government. Accordingly, he believed the armies of the Confederacy could be raised either by voluntary enlistment or through conscription, and in his judgment the legislature alone could determine which method was the more suitable. Here the Attorney General took exception to the belief that Congress could raise armies only through its power to call on the militia to execute Confederate laws, repel invasions or suppress insurrections.

It was also Watts' opinion that whenever the government exerted a delegated power within its own sphere of action, its use of the power should be upheld as the supreme law of the land. Inconsistently, he held that the central government had no sovereign powers,[14] but the context of his opinion indicates he was using the term "sovereign powers" in the sense of that ultimate power which is sovereignty itself. If the central government could be supreme within its own sphere of action, then the position that the states alone retained sovereign powers was untenable. In practical situations the general government decided on the limits of its own sphere of action, and in doing so it was sustained by the supremacy clause. Did the individual states retain their sovereignty intact under the circumstances? Was not the Richmond government autonomous within its own area of activity?

In several instances the Attorneys General upheld Congressional acts which the states sought to obstruct. The vigor with which these Richmond officials supported the government was demonstrated when it began to set up distilleries in the states. In one case a Virginia court had issued an attachment ordering the county sheriff to take possession of the government's distillery, and it had directed that criminal proceedings be initiated against the Confederate officials in charge. Following John Marshall doctrine, George Davis held that Virginia, "in common with her sister States," had recognized the Confederate Constitution as the supreme law of the land, and in his opinion this law superseded all other conflicting laws — meaning those of the states.

Continuing further, Davis declared that since Congress could raise and support armies in the "fullest and broadest terms," it could manufacture whiskey for medicinal purposes. To permit a state to obstruct any one of the steps involved in Congress' supporting the armies would intimate that it could logically obstruct them all. His next point was concise: "Of what avail is this power if it can be easily rendered nugatory by State legislation?"[15] He reasoned that if the states could inhibit the making of whiskey, they could do the same with arms manufacture and the enlistment of men. If they could take all these actions, the "whole war power of the Confederate Government would be prostrate at the feet of the State legislatures."

In another case the Attorney General gave his opinion that a governor could not prevent the building of a Navy distillery by claiming it violated state law. Said he: "I can see no foundation whatever for any authority in a State thus to obstruct the action of the Government." Davis emphasized that the Constitution granted Congress the power to "provide and maintain a navy," and since a state could not inhibit the implementation of this power by forbidding the construction of ships within its boundaries, it could not oppose the distillation of whiskey. According to him, this power and others were "intended to be beyond the control of the States, and they must be so," or else they would become a "mere nullity." Supposedly, then, the general government was autonomous within its own sphere of activity.

An interim Attorney General, Wade Keyes, dealt with a Virginia law which forbade the making of any contract to manufacture whiskey in the state. It was Keyes' opinion that the government could negotiate the contract even in violation of Virginia law, and in outlining his position to sustain Richmond, he combined the power to raise armies with the necessary and proper clause. To carry out its power to raise armies, Congress could use "any means" necessary and proper to obtain needed supplies.[16] In his opinion the government could employ agents to buy the product in foreign countries, and it could establish factories and employ people to make it. Said he: "There is no principle of public law which expressly or impliedly prohibits the Confederate Government from manufacturing powder within a State, nor any which prohibits the citizens of a State from contracting with the Confederate Government to manufacture it within the limits of a State."

Since the contract between the government and state citizens providing that the latter make whiskey would be a legal one, later action by the state could not render it a "nullity." For a government to nullify the contract would suggest it had violated the 1861 Constitution, under whose provision no state could pass a law impairing the obligation of contracts.[17] He concluded that the people of each state joined with those in others "to confer on the central government exclusively all the powers necessary for securing the common good." Whenever Richmond exercised one of these powers, it remained supreme *vis a vis* the states.[18]

Several questions are in order: What was happening to the "sovereignty" of the "independent" states of the Confederacy? Where did sovereignty lie when the creature, the general government, was given a higher constitutional status than the states, its creators? Was not sovereignty itself divided between the "nation" and the states? Years before Jefferson had been troubled because he believed the Washington government was being placed above its creators, the states. Now, the same development which he had found objectionable under his federal experience was being repeated in the Confederacy. War was a compelling reason for concentrating powers and authority at Richmond, but as a consequence there was a certainty that the states' rights spirit of the 1861 Constitution was going to be debilitated in practice.

With few exceptions the legal actions of state courts sustained Richmond's activities, but this condition was foreseeable in the Confederate States, as both Confederate and state judges cited United States precedents in reaching decisions. Both used John Marshall-approved reasoning to support the general government within its own area of activity. As Moore has stressed, the state judges "bolstered up the Confederate government . . . with the irrefragable opinions" of Marshall.[19]

On more than one occasion Richmond officials were, nevertheless, disconcerted by state court decisions unfavorable to the government; still, they sought to obviate their effects by declining to accept these decisions as binding in another case or in another state. Within a particular state the government would "live with" adverse court decisions, while in others officials would "interpret the laws to their liking."[20] Because Confederate district courts could not effectively exercise appellate jurisdiction over state courts, Richmond would initiate prosecutions in these courts, the expectation being that Confederate legal actions would command more popular respect in them.

The extent to which state supreme courts entertained constitutional questions differed from one area to another. The Virginia court of appeals decided only two cases which had constitutional implications; only one was dealt with by the South Carolina court. Out of 19 decisions made by the Mississippi court, just one had a constitutional bearing; both the Florida and Texas courts rendered three constitutional decisions. Tennessee's court made none, but the Georgia, North Carolina and Alabama courts frequently entertained these questions.

In one aspect or another most constitutional questions dealt with the government's conscript power. That cases questioning the legality of conscription should have been brought before state supreme courts was ineluctable, for there were those who believed no act could "more completely display the tyranny of a Consolidated government" than conscription.[21] Yet constitutional decisions basically affecting the government's power to conscript did sustain Richmond.

Upholding the validity of Confederate conscription, the Texas court held that the power to wage war "necessarily included, unless expressly withheld, the right to demand compulsory military service" from citizens.[22] In a Georgia case the petitioners argued that Congress could raise armies only through voluntary methods or by calling out the militia, their contention being that the Confederate draft violated the state's sovereignty. Disagreeing with the petitioners, the court maintained that Congressional powers to raise an army and call forth the militia were separate and unrelated, and it held that the legislative power over conscription was without limit. The court went on to say that the constitutional language used in the raise and support provision "could not express a broader, more general grant of a specific power." Besides, the opinion of the court was that even if the raise and support provision did not authorize the power to conscript, that power could be found in the necessary and proper clause.[23] According to the judicial body, the Richmond government could conscript whenever it decided that voluntary methods were inadequate. In the case of *Burroughs* v. *Peyton* the Virginia court held that without conscription "neither liberty nor national life" could be sustained, and it asserted that the power of conscription remained with the central government, which had a primary responsibility for national defense.

As military defeats increased in number, the government expanded its conscriptive power to involve more citizens, and with the passage of additional laws more court cases were initiated. When an 1864 act terminated the exemption which had been given those draft eligibles who furnished substitutes, the dockets of the state supreme courts were filled. After enactment of the law the principals, those who had had substitutes perform their military obligation, claimed it violated the contract made between Richmond and themselves.

Court attitudes toward the contract were generally favorable to the Confederate position. Alabama's supreme court would not concede that anything more than a "legislative contract" had existed between the principals and the government. It decided that the contract had an "implied condition that any succeeding legislature, acting in good faith . . . should have the power to repeal it." For their part, the principals argued that by taking the substitute Richmond had made an inviolable contract with them, but the court concluded that what the legislature could contract with an individual conscript, it could also revoke. In a Virginia decision the supreme court decided that the constitutional clause forbidding the impairment of contracts could not be used to restrict Congress' authority . Said the court: "No right . . . has been conferred on the government to divest itself, by contract . . . of the power of employing . . . the whole military strength that has been placed at its disposal." [24] The judges decided no contract had existed and that even if it had, the government could have impaired the contract. A Georgia case centered around the petitioner's claim that a contract existed between the conscript and the person who substituted for him. In this case the court concluded that all exemptions were "conditioned, *ex gratia* and not *ex debito justitiae*." [25] This is to say the government made exemptions out of its grace and could not be bound legally to continue them.

That not every court justice considered the contract severable by the general government when occasion required it was clear, for Chief Justice Richmond M. Pearson of the North Carolina court averred that a binding contract had been effectuated. His opinion was that Congress had no right to violate a contract, since the Constitution failed expressly or impliedly to authorize such a violation. Considering the act illegal, Pearson issued writs of habeas corpus to discharge principals held by Confederate enrolling officers. What his actions did was to embarrass the government; however, the full membership of the state supreme court eventually overruled Pearson's opinion about the nature of the contract, upholding the validity of the Confederate law.

As the war continued, the government became perturbed by the actions of inferior court judges who would issue writs of relief for persons who they believed had been apprehended wrongfully by Richmond officials. An 1864 circular of the conscript bureau urged that civil court decrees be honored in individual cases, but that the decree of a particular court should not serve as a guideline for action by conscript officers in other cases. According to the circular, the officers were to "look to the Confederate government for the construction of its laws." [56] Later in the year the Secretary of War sent a letter to the commander of reserves in Mississippi, pointing out that the department could not be bound generally by the decision of a single court.

Additional court disputes developed when Congress enacted a law in 1864 authorizing governors to exempt those persons who they believed were essential to the administration of their governments. In a Georgia case the court held that a person who had won election as an officeholder should be entitled to exemption; its reasoning was that the government had the prerogative to determine what citizens should be elected to public office. At the same time the court maintained that a state could not require Confederate tax assessors to fill militia ranks, when the militia was called out to repel invasion, since neither the general government nor the state could impede the administrative operations of the other. During this period the Virginia supreme court declared Congress had no authority to force state officers into Confederate military service.

Meanwhile, courts in North Carolina, Alabama and Georgia considered ancillary questions, which affected the liability of persons exempted from Confederate service for militia duty. The persons involved were bonded-exempts or plantation overseers who gave the government provisions in return for their exemption from duty. In the Georgia court it was argued that the exempts were in Confederate service and could not be obligated to do militia duty, but the court decided the law granted exemption from Confederate military service only and that Congress had not intended to extend it to militia duty. The Alabama court held that Congress could draft persons for other than military duty and that the state claim to a person's service had to "yield to the conflicting claim of the Confederate States." In this case the court agreed that if a conflict occurred between Richmond and the states, it had to be resolved in favor of the general government. Concomitantly, the court decided that since the 1864 act permitted a large number of exemptions, the statute did not anticipate the releasing of these persons from militia duty.

A Mississippi case involved a question as to whether a state could put its citizens into the militia before their being conscripted by the Confederate government, and if it could claim its citizens when called by Richmond. The opinion of the court was that since the Confederate Constitution and laws were the supreme law of the land, the state's authority in matters of concurrent jurisdiction was inferior. Its justices declared that whenever the government exercised a power given it, its "actions thereon became paramount and exclusive, whether a state had previously acted on the subject or not." [27]

Although the constitutionality of the Confederate habeas corpus act *per se* was never considered by a state supreme court, subsidiary questions relating to the act were entertained. In one case a Confederate enrolling officer in Georgia refused to accept a writ issued by a court, maintaining that since the petitioner had already been enrolled, he, the petitioner, had to take his case before a Confederate court. In considering the question the Georgia court attempted to demarcate the dividing line between sovereignty and political power. Its members held that both Georgia and the general government had political power, but that sovereignty remained unimpaired in the people of each state; yet they admitted that within the scope of its delegated powers, Richmond had to be given an 'implicit obedience." That this was judicial bias designed to meet the states' rights predilections of the jurists was plain, for the difference between giving implicit obedience to a government and acknowledging the sovereignty of another is a narrow one.

In order to influence legal questions relating to issuance of writs of habeas corpus, North Carolina judges and courts insisted on having a concurrent jurisdiction with Confederate courts. In particular they wanted jurisdiction over inquiries made to determine cause of arrest by Richmond officials.. What the state supreme court contended was that North Carolina judges had the right to issue writs for persons who they believed were being held illegally by Confederate officers. Agreeing with this court, the Georgia justices maintained also that in habeas corpus cases the plaintiff should have the right to decide whether to take his complaints to a Confederate or state court. The implication was that the plaintiff would have better treatment in the latter court, and this was demonstrably the situation in North Carolina, where Pearson issued numerous writs, insisting that the conscript who provided a substitute could not be drafted.

Confederate relations with the Chief Justice deteriorated to the point where it was necessary for President Davis to intervene. Averring that he would "not shrink from the issue," the Executive declared he would intercede if "Pearson tried to imprison Government officers" who refused to honor his writs. One deleterious result of Pearson's actions was that local state courts were encouraged to release conscripts and deserters "if there was a shadow of an excuse for such action." Eventually, Confederate enrolling officers had no recourse other than to treat the lower court orders as of no effect.

Expectedly, Confederate impressment also became a matter of judicial concern. The Georgia court questioned that an arbitrarily fixed scale of prices provided a measurable standard for determining the value of impressed goods. Members of the court argued that the value should be determined at the time of impressment, thus compelling the government to pay the market price. In the case of *Hill v. Cummings* the court acquiesced in the validity of the impressment law, but it would not condone the implementation procedures outlined in the act, as the court decided there had not been provided an adequate compensation for the seized goods. In another case a railroad company sought to enjoin Confederate impressment agents from taking its property; its officials contended that expropriation of its property would impair a contract, since the property in question was mortgaged. But it was the opinion of the court that Richmond's use of its eminent domain power could not compromise the obligation of a contract. Its members emphasized that in every contract there were conditions, one of which was the chance that domain power might have to be invoked by government.

One scholar has written that by middle 1864 the state courts had "fully accepted the military power of the Confederacy"; by this time even Justice Pearson had "yielded in good faith to their decisions." [28] Another has maintained that the tendency of state courts was to "sustain the acts of the Confederate government and not to emphasize states' rights.

Even in the Confederacy the supremacy and necessary and proper clauses of the 1861 Constitution proved elastic under judicial expansionism. There were concerns of secondary importance on which the state courts differed as they interpreted the validity of Richmond's actions; however, the supremacy of the general government within its own sphere of action was sustained. Probably, there was a certain inevitability about judicial support given Richmond, for jurists remained loyal to the federal system of jurisprudence.

Under a federal system of government it is essential that the legitimate functions of the general government are supported judicially. This substantiation can come from state courts as well as those of the central government, but if the general government is not given support in most cases, it is at a loss to carry out national goals. State courts in the Confederacy did not favor their own governments in preference to Richmond; bound by oath to support the Confederate document, their judges did acknowledge the supremacy of the central government. It seems clear that the constitutional division of powers between Richmond and the states was not put into disequilibrium by court decisions of the later. In practice most judicial work was carried on as it had been under the Union.

CONFEDERATE - STATE RELATIONS

The continuing impact of war fostered the expansion of new governmental activities by Richmond, and there developed, concomitantly, a contest between the general and state governments over the constitutional powers to be exercised by each. In this ensuing struggle the principal differences between them centered on conscription, impressment, writ suspension and regulation of foreign commerce.

As the military situation became more serious for the nation, there occurred a centralization of powers at Richmond, and in the process the central government began to exercise an authority whose influence was centripetal. This is to say that the center of political power gravitated toward the general government. Confronted by a prolonged war, the government had to exert more and more controls over the people as a whole, its operations directly affecting individuals within the several states. Because the government assumed more of a centralist role, the result was that the constitutional ascendancy of the states declined. Patently, Confederate interests were singularly threatened after Gettysburg, and during the next two years the government exercised its powers more completely, doing so in a manner that caused the states to become solicitous about the trend of relations between them.

In order to enable the government to prosecute a war, a series of steps was taken early in 1861 by the legislature and President Davis. The Executive began by informing Congress that United States war material held by the states should be placed under Confederate control. In February Congress conferred on Davis the power to "assume control of all military operations" in the states which related to questions between them and the north.[1] In addition, the Executive was authorized to receive into Confederate service whatever troops might be tendered by the state governments. These forces could volunteer for 12 months, provided they obtained the consent of their government; formed as part of the provisional army of the Confederate States, they were placed under Richmond's jurisdiction.

During the next few months many states units were transferred to the Confederate army, units such as the "Provisional Army of Tennessee," which was transferred to general service and became part of the army commanded by Major General Leonidas Polk at Memphis. In Texas camps of instruction were established, and recruits were trained in them for Confederate military duty. Under prodding by Governor Francis R. Lubbock, these troops "were transferred as rapidly as possible" to Confederate service.[2] Forces like these were received by Richmond with their officer ranks already filled and their units organized; however, the Executive was given authority to appoint their general officers.

Serving constitutionally as commander-in-chief, Davis was authorized by a March 1861, law to "employ the militia, military, and naval forces" of the Confederate States, and to call for and accept volunteers totaling not more than 100,000 men, who were to serve for a period of 12 months. In the case of the latter they were called to "repel invasion" and "secure the public tranquility and independence" against "threatened assault." Two months later the President was allowed to receive such units as might tender their services for an indefinite period, and he could take this action "without the delay of a formal call upon the respective States." Because hostilities were commencing, Davis was given authority to use the "whole land and naval forces in the prosecution of the war." During this same period the President was authorized to receive "without regard to the place of enlistment" as many volunteers as he believed necessary;[3] furthermore, he was given the right to appoint the field and staff officers required to command units formed from these volunteers. The relevant point here is that Richmond took the initiative in building its own armed forces, and never relinquished its control over troops representing the general government.

Early in the conflict there were two methods by which a person could join the Confederate army: he could volunteer directly into it or join as a member of militia units as they were tendered by the governors. Whatever the method of enlistment, large numbers of men did come into general service. By the end of this year the contributions of Georgia and Arkansas had reached the respective totals of 25,000 and 30,000 men. Sixteen regiments and seven battalions had joined the Confederate service from Louisiana, other states having made equally impressive contributions.

It was in this initial period that the governors revealed apprehension over the adequacy of their states' defenses. They had reason to attend to these defenses, for even in 1861 the Union was attacking the Confederacy at strategic places along the eastern seaboard and was establishing bases on southern territory. Another factor that caused their concern was that the states had already sent supplies and men to the army of the general government. At one time citizen petitions were sent to the governor of North Carolina urging him to provide better defenses for the eastern part of the state, but Henry T. Clarke had to tell the secession convention that the government had "conveyed to the Confederacy all its troops, arms, arsenals . . . and forts." [4]

Broad executive powers inhered in Davis, who assumed the role as commander-in-chief of Confederate forces and of the militia when called into general service. Because he firmly retained his powers, it was inevitable that he should have incurred the antipathy of an extreme states' righter like the governor of Georgia. At the outset Joseph E. Brown was agitated by Richmond's refusal to accept troop units of larger than regimental size. His expectation was that if Richmond accepted the larger units, he would be able to make appointments to the higher militia ranks, but "he was soon to learn" that the President would not condone enlargement of Brown's appointing power at his own expense. [5] Brown also questioned the validity of a Confederate law which authorized Davis to receive troops without first calling on their states for them; however, he eventually accepted a legislative resolution which provided for the transfer of Georgia volunteer forces into Confederate service.

Although the governor remained a political "troublemaker" for Davis through most of the conflict, Brown's intransigence was frequently more apparent than real, as there were times when he cooperated with the government. Early in the second year the Georgia Attorney General called for a cessation to state recruiting activities so there would be "no interference" with the requisition from Richmond. When Congress authorized the Executive to call on the governors for more militia, Brown established his own informal draft to meet his state's quota, and under his orders any county that failed to supply its men for the Confederacy was subjected to his own draft, which he had initiated on his authority. Whatever the circumstances of the Davis-Brown conflict, Georgia exceeded its quota by 10,000 men.

In 1862 the Confederate Congress, wanting to retain the 12-month volunteers in service in the realization of a long war, enacted the first conscription law in American history, a situation which was ironic in that it was initiated by a union of sovereign states. Entitled an act to privide for the public defense, the statute gave Davis exclusive control over all male citizens between the ages of 18 and 35. What gave the act an urgency to Confederate citizens was that the government could involuntarily enroll them and place them in the service of the central government.

Most vocal in opposition to conscription was Brown, and during most of this year he and Davis participated in a "long-drawn and rancorous pen duel, which finally resolved itself into a mere sparring over the meaning of words."[6] The governor was distressed by the intent of the law to obviate the use of state governments in the enrollment of men and its substitution of a direct call by the general government for one made through the individual state governments. Paradoxically, Brown himself resorted to his own draft without legal authorization; yet he believed Confederate conscription was a "bold and dangerous usurpation by Congress of the reserved rights of the States . . ." He asserted that conscription signalled a "rapid stride toward military despotism," and indicated he could not "consent to commit the State to a policy" which was "subversive of her sovereignty." Despite his protestations to the contrary, the governor submitted to the first conscription act; hoping that his government's "fidelity to the cause" would be unquestioned, he even agreed to the conscription of all men except his civil and military officers.[7]

In their correspondence the President responded to Brown's argument that conscription was invalid by referring to Congress' power to raise and support armies. In Davis' opinion this power enabled the national legislature to decide what method of raising an army would be most effective. As far as he was concerned, whenever Congress exercised this power, it was the sole judge as to whether the legislation intended to carry out the power was necessary and proper. His belief was that conscription was necesary and proper to implement the power to raise and support armies. Concluding his argument, Davis would not agree that constitutional provisions relating to the militia referred "in the remotest degree to the armies of the Confederacy." The Executive, constitutionally secure, held that the governors could appoint militia officers, but that Congress alone had the power to organize, arm and discipline the militia.

Opposing Davis, the governor averred that the constitutional provisions granting Congress the power to raise armies referred to the "whole militia of all the states."[8] The President countered that while the militia could be called into Confederate service, it did not form a part of the armies raised by Congress. What Brown's reasoning did was to lead to the center of the dilemma before the Confederacy, a dilemma revolving around the issue of states' rights versus national interests within a system based on the sovereignty of the states. If

Davis had admitted the armies of Richmond constituted all the militia, then his legal position would have been weakened. But he argued that there was an army called the Confederate, which was separate and distinct from the militia. Davis emphasized, too, that he had called "not for the 'whole militia of all the States,' not for any militia, but for men to compose armies" of the Confederate states. It was his opinion that if one held that Congress could not draft a citizen owing to his membership in the militia, he would "deny the power to raise an army at all." [9]

The President, trying to mollify Brown, did admit that conscription had not been made essential from the standpoint of Georgia's contribution to the war effort, and he expressed his appreciation for the manner in it had responded to calls for troops. He indicated, moreover, his personal indebtedness to Brown for his "prompt, cordial, and effective cooperation." [10] That the governor was a politically agile executive who would issue conflicting statements from time to time was apparent: at one period he intimated in a letter to the Secretary of War that he would not assist in implementing the conscription act; yet at the same time he asserted he would "throw no obstacles in the way of its being carried out." [11]

The governor became more agitated when Congress increased the draft eligible age from 35 to 45 years. Fundamentally, what Brown did not wish to do was to accept the government's activities even when it operated within its legitimate sphere. Above all, the governor opposed the giving of an elastic interpretation to Congress' delegated powers. In this case the governor would not allow the new law to be enforced until the legislature had considered it. Although the latter passed a resolution opposing the principle of conscription, the supreme court decided unanimously in favor of the conscript law, and, finally, the legislature, influenced by Confederate Senator Benjamin H. Hill, committed Georgia to conscription.

Throughout a major part of the war Governor Zebulon B. Vance of North Carolina remained a catalyst of opposition to Richmond. When the general government exercized its war power, he wanted the government to give due consideration to the rights of his state; but in order to have uniformity in the conscript program, the War department refused to honor most of his requests for special treatment. At one period the relations between Vance and Richmond were so tense that the legislature sought to allay any suspicion that North Carolina was hostile to Confederate interests, pledging itself to the "most vigorous *Constitutional*" war policy. [12] Still, Vance's opposition to the use of Virginians and Marylanders in acting officially for Richmond within the state reached such intensity that the government employed state citizens to implement conscription wherever possible.

There were several reason for the governor's contrariness. For one matter his area was removed from hostilities duing the conflict, and it could afford to oppose Richmond. And then, too, states' rights sentiment was prevalent in the eastern parts of the state, while Union support was noticeable in the western sections. The nature of the political milieu compelled Vance to be politically ambidexterous for his own electoral survival; in order to enhance his public image he had to take a stand against the Davis administration. He could, at least, indicate publicly his dislike of having North Carolina brigades in the Confederate army commanded by officers from other states in the new Confederacy.

During the first three years of the war the main body of federal troops stayed in the upper south, and owing to their presence few problems in this area disturbed Confederate-state relations, for northern armies were too near to permit a state to resist Richmond's policies. While Governor John Letcher of Virginia made known his own antipathy for conscription, he did not actively resist its implementation.

The effect of war was less apparent in the lower south; however, when the governor of South Carolina tried to impede execution of the conscript law, Davis responded with decision. He pointed out to the governor that the idea of state's being able to relieve its citizens from Confederate duty was erroneous, and he stressed that Congress' power to raise and support armies, and to declare war would be rendered nugatory by this kind of action. Davis' comment was unambiguous: "If a State may free her citizens at her own discretion from the burden of military duty, she may do so the same in regard to the burden of taxation, or any other lawful duty." His opinion was that such an assertion by South Carolina was "tantamount" to denying the government's right to carry out a delegated power.[13] Despite the governor's ideas, the state's executive council did enforce conscription when it was first enacted by Congress.

In the southwest, Francis Lubbock, governor of Texas, co-operated with Richmond officials, and by early 1863 his government had provided the Confederacy with more than 60,000 troops. He revealed that he did not want to dispute the government "on immaterial points," and remarked: "In military matters there should be one sole head. Under the Constitution and laws I recognize President Davis as that head . . ." The governor went on to say that while Davis conducted his administration in conformity with the 1861 Constitution, the President should be "sustained by the officers, both State and Confederate, and by the people." [14] In the middle of the war he sought to assuage any concern on the part of other governors in the area that Richmond would disregard their Trans-Mississippi territory. That he succeeded in his mission was demonstrable, for the governors of Arkansas, Missouri, Louisiana and Texas reaffirmed their support of the general government. Holding conscription to be valid, Lubbock offered the aid of his state government in carrying out the law.

Confederate conscription won endorsement, too, from Governor Henry T. Clarke of North Carolina, Vance's predecessor in office. Early in the conflict the governor declared his intention to "carry out the conscription act fairly and to the fullest extent of the wants of the country." [15] Under his leadership the state's contribution to the cause was impressive; by August, 1862, North Carolina had provided the government with more than 64,000 volunteers.

In evaluating the pattern of relationships between Davis and the governors it would be inaccurate to emphasize the executives, including Vance, Brown, Pettus and Murrah, who opposed the government's conscription program. For the governors of South Carolina, Louisiana, Mississippi, Florida and Texas, Bonham, Allen, Clark, Milton and Lubbock, all co-operated with Richmond. Governor Milton of Florida believed resistance to the Confederate war program would compromise the "honor and dignity of the State in her obligation to her sister States . . ." Writing to Governor Brown, Milton said: "It is best therefore . . . where it can be honorably done, to avoid all conflicts and competition between the State and Confederate authorities for political power." [16]

Policy support for conscription was not possible from the Vice President, Stephens, who declared the draft was "resorted to from no necessity whatever." In his opinion the people were "perfectly willing" to fight for their liberties. [17] What the Vice President did not realize was that the government required conscription to encourage the volunteer spirit. Removed from immediate governing responsibility, Stephens could remain aloof from the problems of the central government, but Davis could not.

A question ancillary to that of conscription, namely, the control of officer appointments in the Confederate army, was the crux of another contest between Richmond and the states. Under the first conscript law the original 12-month servicemen were given the right to select their own officers; then Congress passed a measure providing for the discharge or demotion of officers who failed to pass definite efficiency tests. If the resulting vacancies could not be filled by promotion from the next lower grade, the President was authorized to make appointments on his own. Although the new appointees had to come from the same states as the units they commanded, this law gave Richmond the instrument to exercise control over officer appointments. Under later amendments to the conscript law, state regiments in the Confederate army were denied the right to elect their officers.

When in 1863 a colonelcy became vacant in the fifty-first Georgia, the War department approved an appointment made by the local field comamnder. Governor Brown, opposing the action, contended that since the unit had gone into service before passage of the conscript law, it was still part of the militia whose officers were appointable by him. In response to the governor the Secretary of War declared the regiment was no longer "in any sense" subject to the jurisdiction of Georgia.[18] Constitutionally, the Secretary was secure: since the Montgomery framers had used the exact language of the 1787 document in writing provisions relating to the militia, such forces could not be made subject to state control, whenever they went into general service. In this situation, the central government pursued a policy that would have been followed by a Washington administration.

2

State concern over retaining officials to administer the government and over keeping enough men for local defenses led to further power contests with Richmond. The nature of the struggles differed from one state to another, and its intensity depended on the extent of manpower shortages in each. In 1863 Congress authorized the governors to exempt from Confederate service those officials who they considered were essential to the "due administration of the government." Some governors abused the law, while others stayed within the law's intent and exempted only the minimum number they believed was necessary.

One governor who broadly interpreted the statute was Vance, who exempted militia officers, justices of the peace, town police and operatives working in factories under government contract. At one period the legislature enacted a law exempting blacksmiths, millers and others from military duty; this law was contrary to Congressional statute, but what the Congress did was to enact a measure exempting such persons from duty. While Vance exempted a large number from

Confederate service, his state made a substantial contribution to the cause by providing the Confederacy with 126,000 men before the war's end.

Governor Brown was another who gave a wide interpretation to the Confederate law, for he claimed exemption for all officers of the state, "civil and military, appointed under the laws." [19] Just a month prior to enactment of the law authorizing exemptions, Brown had written to Davis: "I trust . . . I am incapable of factious opposition to the head of an able and vigorous administration, on account of differences of opinion on a few points." [20] Because Georgia remained beyond the battlelines through most of the war, the governor could afford to indulge in his recalcitrance.

When Richmond tried to encourage the governors to reduce the number of their exemptees, additional conflict ensued. Vance was disquieted by the conscription of local judges, for he believed an "annihilation of state rights" was a consequence of their enrollment. [21] Early in 1864 Governor Clark of Mississippi criticized Richmond for its forcing justices of the peace into Confederate service, even though they had been exempted by him. Eventually, the legislature passed a resolution asserting it would relinquish claims to all officials not named specifically in the constitution. Later in the same year the Alabama and South Carolina legislatures declared state officers were no longer subject to Confederate conscription. Since militia officers between 18 and 45, justices of the peace, notaries and constables were still liable to the draft, their actions were inimical to a Congressional statute. But by this year it mattered little what they did to obstruct Richmond, because the Confederacy was near collapse.

According to the Confederate conscript bureau, 25,892 men were certified by their governors as necessary to administration: the numbers included 14,675 from North Carolina, 8,229 from Georgia and 1,422 from Virginia. In the remaining states comparatively few men were granted exemption from duty by their governors; for example, by May, 1964, only 600 had been exempted by the governor of Florida. It appears the number of exemptees exceeded that required to maintain the governments; nevertheless, to argue that if these personnel had been in the Confederate army the war would have taken a different turn is speculative at best.

That controversies between Richmond and the states should have developed over disposition of militia forces was unavoidable, because the governors, apprehensive about their local defenses, were reluctant to relinquish militiamen to the Confederacy. After the initial period in the war when militia units were tendered to Richmond, the governors wanted to retain the remainder intact for local defense purposes. Some governors like Brown proved unresponsive in spite of the government's importunities that militia officers be released for Confederate duty. Others like Clark of Mississippi were willing to give up their militiamen to the general government with a minimum of friction. Comprehensibly, the question of militia control became more serious in the second half of 1864, when federal troops began their pincer movements into Georgia and Virginia.

Although the War department ruled at the outset that militia officers between 18 and 35 were subject to conscription, it deferred to Brown's protest against their being conscripted and the department exempted those "in commission." Writing to Davis late in the second year, the governor protested that his people would not "yield their sovereignty to usurpation," declaring that Georgians would expect the central government, the common agent of all the states, "to move within the sphere assigned it by the Constitution." [22]

Periodically, the Executive found it pragmatic to make minor concessions to the governors. When Governor John J. Pettus of Mississippi requested authority early in the war to organize rangers with over-age recruits, his request was granted by Richmond. Later, the governor, apprehensive about the Confederacy's slowness in assembling forces in Vicksburg, tried to keep the militia together, and he was supported by the legislature which provided that these troops could serve under Confederate army officers, but only for short periods of time. After having used state troops to defend Vicksburg, Pettus declined to co-operate with Confederate officers, when they wanted to remove conscripts from these units later in 1863. His successor in office, Charles Clark, retained, however, only a few thousand cavalrymen in order to assist Confederate units in protecting the state against enemy raids.

Since the war went on, the governments continued to lose their militia to the Confederacy. In 1863 Governor Shorter of Alabama ordered militia from certain counties to muster and defend Mobile; unfortunately, there "was no longer any militia." [23] By the end of the conflict the state had sent almost all the men it could muster for Confederate service, as even small units composed of recruits not liable to Confederate service were taken bodily into government duty by enrolling officers.

Of immediate importance to the governors was the Congressional act passed in February, 1864, which lowered the conscript age to 17

and increased it to 50 years. Under provisions of the law those men
below 18 and above 45 were to form a Confederate reserve for local
defense within the states; however, these forces were to be placed
under the jurisdiction of Richmond. What agitated Brown was that
successive amendments to the original conscription act both lowered
and raised the conscript age, and this condition interfered with his
attempts to retain the Georgia militia intact. Although the governor
tried to organize his militia with men between 16 and 60 who were
not in Confederate service, the legislature voted to turn it over to
Richmond.

Following passage of the February law the governors began to
pursue a more independent course. Since Union forces were moving
closer to the deep south, there was reason for the governors to give
priority to their own states' defenses. Understandably, conflict between Richmond and the states occurred again when Confederate
generals in command of reserves attempted to enroll reservists found
with state defense units. The governors held that these troops were in
essence "troops of war" and should not be taken under Confederate
conscription, but since these units contained derelict conscripts and
many reservists, and were not in permanent military service, the War
department treated them as militia.[24] Despite the requests of some
governors that they be allowed to retain companies of these forces as
organized militia, the Secretary of War would not acquiesce.

The problems which Richmond encountered over this issue varied
from one state to another. Governor Clark of Mississippi for one
came to acknowledge the loss of his troops of war.[25] But in Texas,
Governor Murrah attempted to keep together organizations of his
troops, and he was confronted by General J. B. Magruder, who declared that if the governor persisted on his "extreme State-rights
construction of the laws of Congress," he would have to take the
"consequences." The implication of Magruder's statement was that he
was ready to use force to frustrate Murrah's plans for the troops.
What happened was that the governor retreated from his original
position, which was weak since his troops contained derelict conscripts
subject to Congressional laws.[26]

Because Brown had contested with Richmond throughout the war,
the Secretary of War determined in 1864 that a course of firmness
should be used in dealing with him. It was Secretary Seddon's opinion
that the governor's claim for exemption of militia officers within
conscript age, more local officials and details for industry could no
longer be acceded to. And he ordered Colonel W. M. Browne, Con-

federate officer in charge of conscription in Georgia, to insist on the law's enforcement. Browne was urged to inform the governor that if he tried to compromise his (Browne's) authority as conscript officer, the issue would have to be "distinctly made and met before the people" of the state.[27] The implication was that Richmond would have taken the issue of the governor's obstructionism directly to the people.

At the war neared its end, relations between Davis and the governor reached a breaking point. In one situation the President would not permit General Nathan B. Forrest to move around Sherman's army in Georgia to enable him to strike at federal supply lines. Angered, Governor Brown suggested that Davis' information concerning the relative strength of the federal and Confederate armies was unreliable, whereupon the President responded by saying that most individuals in the governor's position "would not assume to decide on the value of the service to be rendered by troops in distant positions."[28]

Even though the Confederate military posture was grave, the governor would not put his militia under the full control of Richmond, whose army was now concentrated in the state. While declining to honor the President's request for militiamen, he also criticized Davis' objectives and his "imperial" designs. In the governor's opinion it sounded novel to have officers of a government which was the creature of the states discussing their fidelity to the cause, "the loyalty of the creator to the creature." From the fall of 1864 to April, 1865, the governor was in "vitual rebellion against Confederate authority."[29]

If it is assumed that the governor's actions were destructive to the cause, then another presumption has to follow: if the officials exempted by the executive had been added to the Confederate army, the war's outcome would have been affected materially. If the governor's withdrawal of Georgia militia from Confederate forces in September, 1864, was of major significance, then another presumption must follow: the march of Sherman's army to Charleston, South Carolina, could have been arrested by use of the Georgians. It seems manifest that neither presumption is tenable, because it was only a few months before the Civil War would terminate.

Since the Richmond government sought to require his service, whether or not offered voluntarily, conscription became an urgently personal matter for the individual citizen. How could the situation have been different? The Montgomery framers had used the same language as the 1787 authors in writing provisions relating to the war powers of the general government. These war powers gave Richmond the same range of authority to act on behalf of the people as a whole. It was the central government which could call the militia into Confederate service discipline it, raise and support armies, and maintain a navy. And it was the Richmond government which could call on state officials to recognize the supremacy of the Constitution. Jefferson Davis, no less than Lincoln, was commander-in-chief of the armed forces with all the constitutional precedents that had been incorporated into the power, and he had the obligation to take care that the laws be faithfully executed. In general, the Executive's response was firm, when he believed a Vance or a Brown was encroaching on concerns of national interest.

3

The authority of the central government directly affected the lives of individual citizens when Richmond suspended the writ of habeas corpus, engaged in impressment and regulated commerce. The 1861 Constitution was concise enough on writ suspension: "The privilege of the writ of habeas corpus shall not be suspended, unless when, in case of rebellion or invasion, the public safety may require it." Using its power to authorize writ suspension, Congress granted authority to suspend on three different occasions. Although the total time period for suspension extended from February 1862 to August 1864, it was in force only about eighteen months. Under the initial law suspension covered arrests made by the central government for offenses against the Confederacy. In the last statute relating to suspension, it was limited to cases of treason, desertion, communicating intelligence to the enemy or unlawfully trading with them.

Demonstrably, abuses were committed by Confederate officials as they implemented writ suspension. In June, 1862, General Thomas C. Hindman unilaterally declared Arkansas to be under martial law. To justify his action, he referred to the "virtual abdication" of civil authority and to the "reign of profiteering" which was taking place.[31] The President subsequently forbade unilateral declarations of martial law without his explicit approval; nonetheless, the problem persisted.

States' rights scruples were troubled by suspension of the writ. For his part, the Vice President believed suspension was "not only unwise, impolitic and unconstitutional," but "exceedingly dangerous to public liberty."[32] Declaring that martial law was "nothing but an abrogation of all laws,"[33] he wrote to Governor Brown that every state should "denounce and condemn the wicked act."[34]

Stephens was not alone in condemning its suspension; the Georgia

legislature adopted a resolution condemning it, expressing at the same
time its confidence in the "integrity and patriotism" of Davis.[35] By
early 1864 Brown was revealing his "deep mortification" at the action
of Congress in permitting suspension under the "pretext of necessity."[36]
It was his judgment that Congressional power to authorize suspension
was an implied power, which had to defer to limitations incorporated
into the Confederate bill of rights. Yet Congress was taking a valid
constitutional position when it granted its authorization for suspension; furthermore, the war could not have been carried on unless the
government had been willing to use its powers fully. Believing the
conflict had greater urgency than Brown, Congress generally supported the Davis administration's requests for suspension, at least
during the middle years of the war.

Governor Vance was disturbed by writ suspension, asserting at one
time that the state was in "danger" of being over-run by officials of
the central government. Said a member of the state senate in 1864:
"Instead of a confederacy of free and sovereign States, we have established a most powerful military despotism."[37] Had the Confederacy
become something more than a union of states? Was the Richmond
government subverting the "sovereignty" of its creators by becoming
militarily powerful?

It was in 1863 that the power struggle between North Carolina and
Richmond began to take form; the immediate cause was the state
supreme court's issuance of writs of *habeas corpus* to obtain the release
of persons arrested by Confederate authorities. Vance ordered the
militia not to arrest anyone as a deserter or conscript whose discharge
had been approved by the state judiciary. Countering the governor's
move, the War department instructed Confederate enrolling officers
to "ignore actions" of Chief Justice Richmond Pearson, who was granting the writs.[38] When Pearson continued in his "factious course," Davis
intimated he would intervene if necessary. That the general government should have become exercised by the judge's interpretation of
the conscript law was understandable; however, following the President's stand, "little more" was heard of conflicts between the judiciary
and Confederate conscript officers working in North Carolina.[39]

Palpably, suspension of the writ was not the only point at issue
between the central government and the states, for another power
struggle ensued over the impressment activities of the former. The
basic problem was that producers had to sell their commodities at
a price fixed by government appraisers, and an easy implementation
of the law was complicated because the prices determined under the

aegis of the War department and the governors were below those
of the current market. What impressment amounted to was a form
of indirect taxation; moreover, abusive practices came to be associated with the program: "When carried out legally, impressment
proved to be harsh and unequal in its operation, but when it was not
done according to law, it proved unbearable." [40]

Particularly agitating to the governors were the illegal activities of
persons who posed as Confederate impressment agents. Milton of
Florida complained about the "shameless frauds practiced by im-
posters" in the state, where friction occurred between Richmond
officials and private property owners over impressment — "with the
victory usually for the Confederacy." [41] In neighboring Georgia the
governor urged people to oppose agents who could not show official
authorization for their impressment, and the legislature made illegal
impressment prohibitable by law. In 1864 Governor Brown was ad-
monishing citizens to be on guard against bands of Confederate
cavalry which roamed the state in an unauthorized search for provisions.

The Alabama legislature made it a penal offense to represent oneself
unlawfully as a Confederate impressment agent, and both fines and
imprisonment were attached to the commission of offenses. In Louisiana the governor expressed his opinion that the impressment law was
"most unwise," and the legislature enacted a law providing a fine
and imprisonment for those who impressed property illegally. Legislators protested against what they considered to be the arbitrary
seizure of property under the pretext of not allowing it to fall into
Union control. Eventually, the legislature passed a joint resolution
declaring that Confederate seizures had caused "unnecessary suffering
and destitution to many people." [42]

Both South Carolina and Mississippi were disturbed by Richmond's
handling of the slave problem. Fewer than four months before the
war's end the South Carolina legislature passed a law forbidding any
slaves to be impressed for work outside the state. That this law was
in conflict with existing Confederate law was apparent, for the latter
provided that slaves could be moved to work anywhere in the Confederacy. What the state law did in effect was to nullify a statute
of the general government, but, then, it was now late December, 1864,
and the legislature's action has to be held in perspective. In Mississippi citizens were irritated by what they believed was an improper
handling of the slave situation by Richmond. Because the Union
enlisted Negroes as they came into federal lines, Davis ordered the

Confederate army to transfer slaves from areas accessible to the enemy. In the opinion of Mississippi's governor this kind of policy would "drive" Negroes into federal supervision, and this was the situation that obtained. When Confederate military commanders began moving slaves away from exposed territory, the Negroes fled in numbers to Union lines. Late in the third year the legislature passed a resolution calling on the governor to protect citizens from Confederate impressment of their slaves.

To attempt to make an accounting of the value of all properties impressed by the central government would be a formidable task. Suffice it to say that inflated paper money was used regularly to make purchases through impressment, and by the end of the war there were unpaid receipts totaling about 500 million dollars. Thus, there is reason to assume that the value of impressed properties was high.

Relations between Richmond and the state governments were weakened further when the general government exercised its power to regulate commerce among the states and with foreign countries. At one time the government in South Carolina tried to forbid the exportation of cotton, unless its shipment was approved either by the government or Richmond; what the Secretary of War did was to oppose decisively the action and the restriction was lifted. Given the constitutional power to regulate commerce of an interstate nature, the central government could not have given its acquiescence.

To inhibit abusive practices which were associated with foreign trade, Richmond began to impose restrictions on such trade during the third year. Writing to the President, Governor Milton of Florida spoke of the "villainous" traffic of speculators who were importing liquors but "no arms or munitions of war." The response of Congress was to enact two bills early in 1864 which forbade the importation of specific luxury items and prohibited the export of cotton and other commodities except under regulations of the President.

These regulations enabled the government to collect cotton and other products, and to license their exportation or transport them overseas on its own account. They also provided that vessels exporting any commodity found on the enumerated list had to carry one-half of their tonnage on outgoing and incoming trips for the government. Cargoes were to be carried at fixed rates, and vessels had to return to the government at least one-half of their cargo proceeds in legally imported articles. Besides, Richmond required that ships disclose information pertaining to their personnel, crews and passengers; rev-

enue officers of the government were authorized to inspect ships'
cargoes.

In the beginning private companies assumed the government could
not compel state-owned or chartered vessels to give up any part of
their cargo space to Richmond. As a result, efforts were made to
evade regulations by having the state governments charter ships or
buy shares in them; nevertheless, Richmond enforced the letter of the
law, and only vessels owned by the governments were exempted from
regulations.[43] Definite consequences awaited those ship owners who
declined to give Richmond one-half of their cargo space: they would
be denied clearance from port, and they would be denied products
with which to carry on an export trade. One of the best indices to the
effectiveness of government regulations was a complaint of ship owners
that the "terms imposed" on them "were so onerous as to render impossible the continuance" of their business.[44] Trying to strike against
the regulations, the owners withdrew from trade. Still, the Davis administration contended that only vessels owned outright by the states
would be free from regulations, those ships merely chartered by them
remaining subject to the rules.

Both Georgia and North Carolina decided to test Richmond's determination to uphold the regulations. In 1864 Governor Brown had
a vessel chartered by Georgia loaded with state cotton; when he
requested clearance from the port, he was informed that none could
be had until half of the vessel's space was alloted to Richmond. Cognizant of the extent of Confederate authority, he asserted that the
program was being carried out in "utter disregard of every principle
of state rights and state sovereignty." [45] During this same year the
steamer *Hansa*, owned in part by North Carolina, was detained by
a Richmond official, who pointed out that the ship's cargo failed to
hold the amount of cotton he believed it should. The President,
writing to Governor Vance, commented that by sharing the ownership
and profits with state governments, speculators were seeking to avoid
government regulations, which had to be enforced.

In June, 1864, Davis vetoed a bill which forbade the government
to regulate vessels sailing on state account. Under the measure this
prohibition was to apply to vessels owned in part or in whole by the
state, or chartered by it for its sole use. Consistently, the Executive
rejected any device to exempt from regulations those ships which were
only chartered and not owned by the state governments. And he would
not allow them to take for their "separate use" any part of the half
used by the general government. He stressed that the army in the

field was the Confederate, which the government was obligated to provision. Said he: "The performance of this duty demands the most strenuous exertions and the command of all the resources that can be reached." [46]

Observable benefits accrued to the central government through its regulations of trade: it was able to secure more imports, meet installments due on its foreign loan and terminate the contract system, under which the government had had to pay high freight rates for its own shipping. Primarily at the bidding and urging of the states' rights governors, Congress removed all restrictions over blockade-running in March, 1865; however, by this time there was in reality no "port of consequence from or to which" blockade-running ships might go. Richmond's regulations were stringently enforced as long as they were in effect, and it was inevitable that they should have incurred the dislike of those who believed the central government was becoming inordinately powerful.

4

Endowed with meager industrial and limited manpower resources, the Confederacy managed to remain in the war for nearly four and one-half years. When one reflects on the nature of obstacles before it, one can appreciate the viability demonstrated by its governmental system.

One continuing obstacle was the presence of inhabitants in mountain areas of the south who had not wanted to participate in secession. Union sentiment was, for instance, vocal in the western counties of North Carolina, which had left the federal government with reluctance. At one period discontent with conscription and taxation was so considerable that Governor Vance had to make a personal plea for loyalty to the cause, issuing a proclamation in September, 1863, that called on citizens not to "seek to cure the evils of one revolution by plunging the country into another." [47] A recurring critic of Davis, he affirmed his own allegiance by saying: "The Constitution of the Confederate States and all laws passed . . . are the supreme law of the land . . . So long as these remain upon the statute books they shall be enforced." [48]

Although he had earlier favored the initiation of peace negotiations with Washington, the governor changed his opinion in the middle of 1864, and began to support Richmond with unaccustomed interest. An obvious reason for his changed attitude was his need to run for re-election, and his desire to avoid identification with the peace party headed by his rival for the governorship, William A. Holden, whose followers advocated peace with the Union on the "best terms to be had." [49] To ensure his political survival, Vance opposed the calling of a convention to facilitate peace discussions and recommended continuation of the fighting.

In the last few months moves to negotiate with the north became noticeable. Late in 1864 a resolution was offered in Congress which would have had the states consider peace terms tendered by Washington, but the proposal was defeated by a large margin. Because the 1861 Constitution recognized that only the states retained sovereignty, such a resolution might have been expected to have had minimal difficulty in passage, unless the governmental system had become different from that envisioned four years earlier.

At the state level resolutions were offered, for example, in the Georgia legislature urging the state to initiate independent negotiations with the Union. Responding to the resolutions, President Davis countered that such action by Georgia would "tend to create discord instead of united counsels," and suggested it would indicate to "our enemies the possibility of a dissolution of the Confederacy." [50] At the same time he expressed his belief that only the general government could negotiate with the federal government. In any event, resolutions in the state legislature calling for a convention of the states to begin a peace program failed to win approval, and even as late as February, 1865, the senate was calling for a "vigorous prosecution of the war." Earlier, the governors of Georgia, Virginia, North Carolina, South Carolina, Alabama and Mississippi had pledged their support to Richmond. Although they had become critical of the government, they declared they would help it in raising troops and "otherwise strengthening" its operations. [51]

It is remarkable that the Confederacy was not split apart by the diverse efforts of the states to make separate peace with the north, but the condition was that they held onto their membership until the force of arms compelled dissolution from without. A state's right to secede was never acknowledged specifically in the 1861 Constitution, because this was a document established on the sovereignty and independence of each. Since there was no necessity to reiterate what was constitutionally plain, the states presumably retained the right to withdraw at will — none did so.

5

Consider the changes in the degree to which Richmond asserted its authority and powers. On the one side of an authority-dominance scale there was the government's calling on the governors to provide troops; on the other side there was the central government's forming local units of defense within the states and placing them under its direct control. Effective prosecution of this "modern" war required a larger and larger measure of control centralized at Richmond, and, as the situation became more ominous for the Confederacy, this control had to be expanded further.

Confederate citizens observed the evolution of a general government which could raise armies on its own, call out the militia, regulate interstate and foreign commerce, and impress supplies. When Richmond exercised these powers, it was sustained by constitutional provisions which made Davis military chief, asserted the supremacy of Confederate laws and facilitated the assumption of implied powers. In practice Richmond employed these powers in varying combinations, but the end result was that an expansive interpretation could be given to the constitutional limits reached by the general government. The extent of the totality of power available to Richmond meant that national interests could be supported constitutionally in every facet of the power accretion.

Back in the 1920s Frank Owsley maintained that the governors pursued such a deleterious course in their relations with Richmond that the Confederacy lost the war, and that gubernatorial devotion to state interests worked to the detriment of the Confederate interest. His position that the Confederacy "died of state rights" is untenable, for it is essential to keep the refractory behavior of a Vance or Brown in proper perspective, since both of their governments made impressive contributions to the cause in manpower and supplies. Both men were activist governors who defended the interests of their states; nevertheless, there is reason to assume that a correlation existed between the potency of their opposition and the effectiveness with which Richmond asserted its powers. Because these governors were capable politicians in their own right, they realized their electoral survival depended on their giving public opposition to the process of centralization which was occurring. Since this development was contrary to the spirit of the Montgomery Constitution, it is not unusual that these activists responded.

Admittedly, there were differences in the degree of support given the government by the governors. As we have seen, the resistance of Brown and Vance was pronounced, but the fidelity of Lubbock was just as emphatic; most governors held a position between the two extremes. Despite new Confederate-state tensions in 1864, there is no evidence that any state used its constitutional power to impeach Confederate officials operating within it. If Vance or Brown had wanted to go beyond their public protestations, they had the legal opportunity to do so, but they took no such action.

Under the Confederate experience a constitutional preference for states' rights was altered to one of support for the general government, and in reality the creature was placed above its creators, the states. States' rights had to be subordinated to national rights and responsibilities which Richmond alone could meet. What did occur was that the rights of the states were relegated to a secondary rank in the contemporary hierarchy of political values.

If the south had wanted to withdraw with success, it might have made the move 40 years earlier, when the manpower and economic resources of the two regions were in better proportion. By 1860 the south's advantages *vis-a-vis* the north's were negligible. In practical terms the Confederacy could not even afford military campaigns which were ambitious in nature, although its armies emerged the temporary victors in some battles.

IX

ACTIVITIES OF THE STATE GOVERNMENTS

Underlying the philosophy of the 1861 Constitution was the concept that the states retained their individual sovereignty. Secessionist leaders had opposed the nationalist interpretation of the 1787 document, which facilitated the expansion of national powers; yet they decided to ratify the Confederate Constitution in the same manner that the older fundamental law had been approved. What this development presaged was that the newer would be submitted to state conventions which would more directly represent the wishes of the people than the legislatures. The nationalists in the Washington government, who maintained the conventions of 1787 secured their authority directly from the people as individuals, had claimed there was thus created a direct constitutional link between the people and the national government. Since the Confederacy used generally the same procedure for ratifying its constitution, was there again created a direct constitutional link between the people and the Richmond government?

After having approved the secession ordinances, these several conventions gave post secession definition to state citizenship, and provided for the continuation of administration in the absence of federal authorities. Specifically, the Mississippi convention declared that all citizens of the United States domiciled in its jurisdiction were now state citizens; moreover, it annulled a constitutional provision declaring that an oath of allegiance be taken to the 1787 Constitution. All Mississippi citizens were released from "obligations of fealty" to the Union, the state itself having resumed its prerogatives as a "free, sovereign, and independent commonwealth." Unless there was conflict with the secession ordinance, all rights safeguarded by the United States and state constitutions were to be inviolable. By decision of the convention an office of postmaster general was established, and all federal laws and regulations pertaining to the mail service were re-enacted.

In Alabama the convention passed an ordinance accepting federal laws relating to the value of gold and silver coins, adopted the United States land system, passed a homestead law, accepted most of the Union army regulations for its own forces and adopted the standard

115

system of weights and measures used by Washington. All state laws in force on January 11, 1861, and not in conflict with convention ordinances were to remain unchanged by withdrawal from the Union.

What is significant about these conventions is that they performed both constitutional and legislative functions, but their attempts to entertain more nearly legislative concerns stimulated opposition. In some cases this opposition was minimal; however, in others it was vocal. The crux of the problem was that the conventions not only became involved in legislative matters, but they also sought to restrict gubernatorial powers.

In order to supervise its defenses, the Arkansas convention created a military board to consist among others of the governor who was to serve only as a member of the group with no special authority in decision-making given him. When the South Carolina governor's call for volunteers met with negligible response, the convention determined that his power should be exercised by an executive council to be composed of the governor, lieutenant governor and three other members appointed by the convention. Revealing a lack of confidence in the governor's capacity to govern, the council assumed for itself almost "unlimited war powers." [1]

The executive council's functions proved to be extensive: it was authorized by the convention to make appointments, declare martial law, provide for the manufacture of war supplies and prohibit the distillation of grain. During the second year of war the council administered the first Confederate conscription law and initiated a statewide system to impress Negro labor for use on coastal defenses. Inevitably, the council, characterized as a body of "tyrants and usurpers," [2] was censured for attempting to govern without recognizing the separation of executive, legislative and judicial powers as outlined in the constitution. The problem was finally resolved in late 1862 when the convention re-assembled and decreed the council's end, and the legislature, resuming its own leadership, criticized the body for "its dictatorial rule," and declared all measures passed by the council to be invalid.

After supporting secession from the Union, the Florida convention similarly began to deal with legislative concerns, authorizing the selection of four counselors to confer with the governor. It was not long before the convention's actions incurred the dislike of Governor Milton, who asserted that the convention had "no right" to the powers it took and was functioning as an "extralegal agent outside constitutional restraint." [3]

Although the Alabama governor called the legislature back into special meeting in 1861, the convention continued to enact measures of a legislative nature; its members justified their actions by referring to the emergency requirements of the era. They reorganized the militia, issued state bonds to meet expenditures and provided for the common defense.

The most serious of these political contests between convention and legislature took place in North Carolina, whose convention during its first session passed more than 30 ordinances pertaining to a variety of subjects. It passed ordinances fixing the terms of treason against the state, relieving volunteers from poll tax obligations, providing for the election of members to the provisional Congress and appropriating money for the next biennium. One scholar has suggested that a prevailing belief was that the convention had "accomplished little" that could not have been done by the regular legislature.[4] That the conventions should have become occupied with legislative details was unavoidable, for the war itself had an immediacy about it that required the undertaking of new actions.

To say that the constitutional changes effected in state government were conservative would be accurate, since the war did not foster any marked alterations in the fundamental laws. Each constitution was altered to make it conform to the state's new position in the Confederate States of America; in the 1845 Texas constitution the term "United States of America" was simply replaced by the corresponding "Confederate States . . ." where applicable. Virginia's constitution, framed in the 1850 decade, remained in force through the war; Louisianians changed their document to prevent the legislature from meeting more than sixty days during the regular session. Since this was a period in our governmental past when legislatures were suspect, it was not novel that such a provision was incorporated into the constitution.

The few changes made in the Georgia constitution increased the number of legislators in the senate, called for an annual meeting of the legislature to replace the biennial assembly and required that a convention of the people be called to amend the constitution. Under the old document legislative approval alone was necessary to add amendments to the constitution. Both the new and the old forbade the importation of Negroes from foreign countries; each protected ownership in slaves by requiring that legislative emancipation could come only with the consent of slave owners.

In Alabama constitutional changes limited the annual sessions of the legislature to thirty days and gave the state the right of eminent domain. In addition, the legislature was prohibited from delegating power to individuals or corporations to levy taxes; nor could it levy taxes for the benefit of individuals or corporations under a general law. Nonmilitary debts could not, furthermore, be incurred through action of the legislature unless a large majority of members supported their incurrence. While these changes won approval by the convention, none was submitted to a popular referendum.

Florida's convention reduced the governor's term to two years and allowed for his re-election, and authorized the legislature to impose a tax on land and slaves whose incidence would fall more heavily on nonresidents than on residents. Constitutional amendments were to be made only by a convention whose meeting would be requested by the state legislature.

Confronted by Union forces which were disrupting their administration, Mississippi legislators amended the constitution by "simple resolution as occasion demanded." A statute passed, for example, in 1864 read: "Be it enacted that the constitution of Mississippi be and the same is hereby altered and amended." [5]

Under a federal system it is essential that the states have the power to change their forms of government; constitutionally, these units in the Confederacy remained free to design their own forms.

2

As the dimensions of the military struggle became clearer, the governments recognized the necessity of intervening in their economies. Because new requirements began to emerge, they had to abandon prewar *laissez faire* ideas concerning their participation in the public sector of the economy. Civil and military needs multiplied with rapidity, and the individual governments were compelled to forego their scruples against economic involvements. All evidence indicates the governments did succeed in meeting their nonfiscal responsibilities.

Salt supplies proved to be inadequate, and the governments tried to encourage private companies to make adequate quantities of it. What the Florida legislature did was to grant the privilege of salt-making to the governments and private entrepreneurs of nearby states. This kind of encouragement represented only an inchoate step, as the governments were soon resorting to measures whose objective was a centralization of control over salt supply. In Virginia the government collected most of the salt production, supervised its making and distributed salt to the public at moderate prices. Alabama authorized its governor to take possession of all salt when needed for public use, and established a salt commission to supervise salt works owned by the government in Louisiana. In Georgia the governor ordered all railroads to detain salt shipments not intended for personal use. To justify his position, Governor Brown referred to a constitutional power which permitted seizure of private property for public use, if "just compensation" was given. For its part the North Carolina convention authorized the election of a commission to engage directly in salt manufacture.

In order to stimulate the growing of provision crops, the governments tried to reduce cotton and tobacco production by imposing restrictions on it; by the middle of the war all states except Louisiana and Texas were placing limitations on the planting of either crop. Mississippi, lacking enough staples, requested planters not to cultivate more than one fourth of their normal cotton crop, the expectation being that grain, stock and fruit production would be thereby encouraged. In specific terms the governor asked farmers not to plant more than one acre of cotton for every worker in the field. Central to the problem of control was the fact that high prices were being offered for cotton, and illicit trading with the enemy proved tempting; however, the governor's campaign of persuasion led to an increase in corn production during the year.

Arkansas sought to limit the planting of cotton by restricting production to two acres per field hand; the Georgia legislature limited production to three acres per hand, while Alabama, using its power of taxation, imposed a tax of ten cents per pound on all cotton produced in excess of 2,500 pounds. In Virginia a maximum of 2,500 plants for each hand was placed on the production of tobacco. These kinds of actions represented anomalous authority to be exercised by governments which had followed a *laissez faire* policy in the private sectors of their economies. Although there were administrative difficulties experienced in limiting cotton production, the number of bales did decline from 4,500,000 in 1861 to fewer than 300,000 in 1864.

To safeguard the supplies of corn production, the states tried to prohibit the distillation of corn whiskey. In Florida distilleries under Confederate contract could remain in business only if they registered a bond; rights to distill were forfeited if the company neglected the contract or engaged illegally in private trade. Several Georgia distilleries were seized by the government when Governor Brown ordered the closing of all not under Confederate contract. A Mississippi act of 1864 called on every person to destroy any existing distillery as a "public and common nuisance."⁶ The state's anti-distillery laws were not implemented with conspicuous success, and two public distilleries had to be set up subsequently to manufacture liquor whose products were then distributed by county dispensary agents for medicinal purposes.

The field of domestic manufacturing also commanded the wartime interest of these governments. Late in the war Virginia authorized its governor to establish an agency to buy yarns, cotton and wood cards, and raw cotton, which were to be offered to the public at the "lowest possible" price. The authorization gave the governor the right to requisition cotton cloth or yarn from factories, and to impose fines on factories that would not accede to his requisitions. In Alabama bounties of five and ten cents were offered for all cotton and wool cards; the government itself engaged in the manufacture of clothing, shoes, whiskey and army supplies. Louisiana engaged in the manufacture of cotton cards, and its governor appointed a Josiah Marshall to supervise the construction and operation of card plants at Minden.

At the outset of the war the Georgia legislature appropriated 100,000 dollars to establish a factory to make cotton cards for use in home manufacturing; under the law these cards were to be distributed by county court justices without cost to those unable to pay. As early as 1861 there were 40 cotton and eight woolen mills under contract for North Carolina, and agents traveled through the counties to buy wool and hides, and to expedite their shipment to manufacturers. In Texas a cloth factory whose products were either sold or given gratis to the public was established in the penitentiary.

That the governments should have become involved in the production of arms to meet the demands of war was understandable. To give impetus to arms manufacture, the Alabama legislature took the following actions: it appropriated 30,000 dollars to stimulate the production of saltpeter, sulphur, lead and powder, provided that all patents held under United States laws prior to January 11, 1861, were still in force and re-enacted the federal copyright laws. Louisiana created a mining and manufacturing bureau, whose objective was to choose sites for iron and lead furnaces, and "other works necessary to develop mineral resources" of the state.⁷ Searching for a "god from a machine to save an agrarian economy," Mississippi chartered a munitions factory; moreover, its legislature assured gunpowder makers that their employees would gain exemption from military service.⁸ Arkansas provided 300,000 dollars to assist the manufacture of iron, cotton cards and salt, while Georgia offered a bounty of 10,000 dollars to any person who would set up a cannon factory capable of making three guns per week. The latter's neighboring state, Alabama, long opposed to granting public funds to assist private business, "inaugurated a policy of economic assistance that had neither been foreseen nor provided for in the Constitution." [9]

Following Confederate practices, the governments requisitioned supplies and personnel when the state interest required it. In the second year of conflict Mississippi gave its governor the right to impress workers and buy supplies to fix rail lines. At one period the Alabama governor was allowed to impress leather, shoes, and shoe-making materials for use of the army, and to impress Negroes for work in government industries, such as niter and salt working. In Louisiana the governor could impress male slaves between the ages of 18 and 50 who were to be used to build and maintain military fortifications. In addition, "syndics" were to be appointed by the chief executive in order to work abandoned plantations for the benefit of their absentee owners. A Virginia act of 1862 authorized the governor to issue a call for at least 10,000 Negroes at any time. Patently, it was not only slaves who were impressed into labor service, for Virginia, South Carolina, Mississippi and Georgia allowed the impressment of free Negroes to work on fortifications. In Texas an act of 1864 made all free male Negroes between 18 and 50 eligible for conscription as teamsters or as other workers.

Cognizant of the debilitating effect of illegal blockade-running on their economies, the governments sought to exercise control over it. In Florida law-respecting blockade runners had to secure clearance papers from the governor; these entrepreneurs were often bonded to make certain they would bring back provisions in exchange for the cotton or turpentine they exported. Both North Carolina and Georgia engaged actively in foreign commercial ventures, the latter chartering the direct trade and navigation company with an initial capitalization of three million dollars. Governor Brown was given the authority to charter a line of steamers to export cotton in exchange for needed imports, and purchasing agents were used by the state in Europe to supervise the exportation of clothing and shoes for Georgia troops. North Carolina was no less preoccupied, as it appointed a state cotton agent to purchase, collect and preserve cotton supplies for the government, his job being to move enough cotton to Wilmington so that blockade runners could put it to profitable use.

Just as Richmond more completely used the constitutional powers given it, so did the states move positively into new areas of activity. Required by war to assume a more aggressive role in economic affairs, they proceeded to grant financial aid to business and even manufactured goods on their own account.

3

What impeded the continuation of viable administration was the possibility of Negro uprisings and the recurring presence of federal troops. Apprehension about Negro difficulties was demonstrated in Florida, whose legislature divided the counties into "beats," state officials organizing periods of patrol duty during which time citizens were requested to "watch for negro trouble." [10]

Of more immediate concern was the appearance of Union military forces. Because it had a thinly defended coastline, Virginia seldom experienced any slackening of enemy pressure at one point or another; its administration was disrupted by the on-and-off-again presence of federal troops on its extremities. The Tennessee experience went beyond that of Virginia, since after the Fort Donelson defeat in 1862 the government moved to Memphis, where the legislature adjourned *sine die* in March. The relevance is that organized civil government discontinued all operations, and the governor found refuge with the Confederate Army of Tennessee.

Because it had been divested of its young officials, Mississippi had to carry on its administration with disabled servicemen and older appointees. City governments were disadvantaged, as all officers under 45 years were made subject to conscription. When the government began to undertake new activities, many additional officials had to be appointed, officials such as price commissioners, liquor dispensary agents and a salt commissioner. Unfortunately, some of the officials used their offices for speculative ends, and at one time the situation reached the point where the governor had to urge the courts to conclude their criminal dockets in order to "let the officers and people know" that the the laws were going to be enforced. [11]

In the third year of the war Mississippi's administration became even more disorganized, as Union troops began entering an increasingly larger number of counties. One direct consequence of their presence was that the state's finances were weakened: levee taxes had to be suspended, and tax abatements were given those whose livestock was destroyed through enemy action. As one scholar has put it, the government became a "peripatetic institution" with "no permanent place of rest." [12] Although gubernatorial direction brought continuity in operation, "Mississippi government and politics were exceedingly chaotic." [13]

Equally insoluable-appearing problems of an administrative nature were experienced in other areas. That there were not enough officials to sustain the government of Arkansas was obvious. Late in 1861 Governor Henry Rector found that nearly 50 per cent of the government's civil offices were unfilled. What had happened was that office-holders had enlisted in the military without first resigning, the result being that the governor could not appoint new officials to take offices which were officially unvacated. Prior to Richmond's calling on those men between 17 and 50 for service, the government in Alabama had employed young boys to assist in administering laws, but by the end of the war the administration had become disorganized in at least half of the counties.

North Carolina's experience provided no exception to the problems common to all. Addressing the 1864-1865 legislative session, Governor Vance deplored the lack of law and order in the state, and pointed out that deserters guilty of murder and plunder were roaming many counties. Similarly, Alabama was confronted by army deserters, and legislation was passed that directed officials to aid Confederate enrolling officers in returning runaways to their army units. A law enacted by the Mississippi legislature required militia officers and county officials to assist Confederate authorities in apprehending deserters. Agitated by the depredations of guerrillas in "no man's land," Louisiana used the militia to arrest their plundering. In 1864 the governor was authorized to enlist regiments "to act as conservators of the peace, and for the defence of the State." [34]

Even under the most advantageous conditions the maintenance of a workable administration in wartime is problematic; yet these governments did attempt to mitigate the more dysfunctional influences to the extent they could.

4

In terms of political and economic realities the problem of financing the war proved insurmountable for both the central and state governments. After all, it was one matter of finance a conflict through the issuance of unbacked treasury notes, but it was still another to try to make paper money a workable medium of exchange. Basically, the difficulty was that citizens were unwilling to give the paper notes a general acceptance, the consequence being that each government issued more and more notes. These states demonstrated, moreover, that they were not equal to the task of maintaining a balance in currency, tax and price considerations, and by the third year financial burdens became heavier at a period when military fortunes began to decline.

Financial problems confounded the states as soon as they began their independent existence. Early in 1861 the governments suspended the making of specie payments by banks, as their objective was to hold hard money in order to allow them to buy needed imports from abroad. These initial efforts proved successful, but in another area of concern the governments experienced failure: unlike the 1787 Constitution, the Confederate document did not forbid the states to emit bills of credit, and what happened was that they were encouraged to issue notes backed by neither gold nor silver. During every session of the Florida legislature new and large authorizations were made, illustratively, for the issuance of paper money, which was used for speculative, short-term objects.

An even further deterioration in the currency situation took place when municipalities, corporations and individuals began to issue paper notes. Realizing the seriousness of the problem, the governments tried to give legislative protection to these notes. At least attempts had to be initiated to give an acceptability to them, but the fundamental difficulty was that there existed a relationship between currency stability and battlefield fortunes. After the fall of New Orleans in 1862, public resistance to Louisiana treasury notes increased, and the situation reached such magnitude that Governor Thomas Moore had to order the arrest of persons in some counties who would not accept the notes. In Florida the legislature endeavored to raise the value of notes by imposing penalties on banks that discriminated against them, while the Virginia legislature declared that any bank failing to accept treasury notes would have its own notes made unreceivable for taxes. The Arkansas legislature provided that creditors who refused notes would have proceedings against their debtors suspended until after the war. In spite of these attempts to safeguard the value of notes, the governments found it laborious to implement note laws in practice.

Under the Confederate Constitution the states were forbidden to "make anything but gold and silver coin a tender in payment of debts," yet they violated the prohibition in both spirit and fact. Both Louisiana and North Carolina made notes acceptable for the payment of state and local taxes, as did Mississippi. In Louisiana the governor directed that treasury notes be made acceptable in the satisfaction of all municipal, parish and state taxes; these notes were made redeemable one year after the conclusion of a treaty of peace between the Confederacy and the United States.

In the Civil War period both north and south revealed a reluctance to impose heavy tax burdens. When the Richmond government levied a war tax in the first year of the conflct, Alabama, in common with most of the other states, raised its share of the tax by borrowing funds from banks — only a few met their war tax quotas through taxation.

Preferring to rely on successive issues of paper monies, Florida failed to increase its tax rates throughout the war, but as the conflict went on, other governments introduced various types of new taxes to meet added expenditures, even though the incidence of these taxes was comparatively light. In Alabama the legislature levied a tax on every 100 dollars bought in state or Confederate bonds which were not purchased directly from the governments involved. Georgia enacted a profit and income tax measure, placing a tax on corporation profits exceeding 20 per cent of their investment capital; however, the law was "poorly administered and generally evaded." During the last two years the state allowed city and county governments to levy new taxes.[15]

In order to protect servicemen, the governments passed laws forbidding debtor proceedings to be initiated against them and authorized the suspension of tax payments due the states. By early 1864 Louisiana was enacting its third tax moratorium law, even though its governor was insisting that the government's revenues were not "exigible for her expenditures."[16]

In accordance with the 1861 Constitution, the states were forbidden to enact any law impairing the obligation of contracts; still, with few exceptions they passed debt postponement laws covering the general public. A North Carolina postponement law met judicial opposition within the state when a court held that the statute deprived creditors of a vested right to demand debt payment; defying the court's decision, the legislature proceeded to enact a nearly identical measure again. While the moratorium laws were subjected to judicial restraint in North Carolina and Arkansas, they were "generally operative" throughout the war in the other states. That wartime exigencies compelled governments to take a more flexible approach toward constitutional restrictions was plain.

It proved arduous for these governments to try to collect the taxes owed them by their citizens. Alabama did not even attempt to collect taxes for 1860 and 1861, and Mississippi, Louisiana and Florida joined in suspending the collection of a large part of state taxes. In Georgia the time period for tax payment was extended, but collection was impossible following Sherman's march to the sea late in 1864. By the early part of 1863 enemy penetration in the Gulf coast, Tennessee border and Mississippi river counties of Mississippi inhibited the collection of that state's taxes.

The issue of inflation, which was "fed" by the inordinate number of personal and corporate paper notes in circulation, was never resolved by the governments. While legislation was enacted to discourage paper note issuance, the notes multiplied with destructive effects on Confederate economic processes. North Carolina made the issuance of shinplasters or debased coin an indictable offense, while the Mississippi legislature placed a 100 per cent tax on unauthorized change bills but neglected to restrict the note issues of cities. Arkansas prohibited the issuance of paper notes by individuals and corporations, but allowed banks to put their notes into the market without any limitation as to denomination.

Protests against rising prices were made by governors and legislators; nevertheless, in the administrative confusion of war enforcement measures simply did not work. Even in the first year the Florida legislature prohibited the export of any hogs, beef cattle or provisions of any kind. Not only did it forbid the export of these commodities, but it also established maximum prices for them, the maximum being set at 33 per cent above cost. In 1864 Virginia's governor sought to delimit inflation and speculation in rice by purchasing it on the government's account and distributing the commodity at a minimum price. Mississippians had to live with abusive practices and inflated prices, for a legislature that doubted the legality of a law imposing price regulations would not legislate against extortionate business practices.

Similar constitutional misgivings were not demonstrated by Alabama legislators, who in 1861 imposed a fine and imprisonment on any person buying livestock or other commodities with the intent of causing a scarcity and higher prices. Georgia sought a legislative approach to runaway prices by forbidding speculation in commodities such as wheat and flour, and imposing a penalty on those who speculated in necessities. Although the legislators' attitude was favorable toward regulation, the governor had to report that the law proved to be a "dead letter." [17] In North Carolina speculation in everyday necessities was held to be a misdemeanor; yet the law was "inoperative." [18] Louisiana created a system of government stores, whose function was to sell goods to the public at reasonable prices. From the standpoint of the government the results were encouraging: "It has drawn in from circulation a large amount of State notes, thus increasing the exchangeable value of the remainder, and has supplied our fellow citizens with articles of necessity." [19]

To assist servicemen's families in need, the governments made substantial expenditures. From 1863 to the end of the war one fourth of the white population of Alabama was given aid by the state and county governments; Florida's expenditures reached the point where one noncombatant for every soldier in the field was being supported by the government. In 1862 Georgia authorized the expenditure of 2,500,000 dollars for the relief of soldiers' families; a year later Texas appropriated 600,000 dollars for relief purposes, Mississippi making one million dollars available during 1864.

As currency declined in value, relief was frequently granted in supplies rather than in cash. In Mississippi county commissioners were employed to impress provisions; if they could not find enough in a single county, they were authorized to impress in others. In Texas the responsibility for relief was taken over by the state government, since the counties could not meet the financial burdens involved. By 1863 the government began to make direct appropriations from state funds for relief purposes; the result was the exertion of centralized supervision by the state over the relief work of local administrators.

Indigent families of servicemen were not the only beneficiaries of government financial aid. Even in 1861 the Louisiana legislature was appropriating money to purchase corn and rice, which were to be given to the poor who were affected by the current drought. And then in 1864 the legislature authorized the governor to buy corn to aid families living in areas of "great scarcity." [20] For its part Virginia extended relief to refugees fleeing from territories in the state that had been destroyed by federal armies.

5

It is evident that the requisitions of war made new demands on the state governments, and these demands stimulated a reorientation of political philosophy. Each demonstrated it was prepared to enter new areas of government involvement; each found that constitutional scruples could not stand in the way of larger controls exerted over the economy and its citizens. That the imposition of new taxes, the use of impressment and the employment of citizens in the militia organizations caused individuals to be aware of a new activism on the part of their governments is certain.

War gave impetus to the centralization of state powers just as it did to a similar centralization by the general government. Successful prosecution of the war from the standpoint of the state governments required additional "state presence" in order to retain the fidelity of their citizens.

The constitutional powers given these governments were substantial, and their leadership, generally speaking, did not neglect to use them. A federal system makes it essential that the constituent units have powers of substance, and this requirement was fulfilled in the Confederacy.

Also, a federal system requires that each state remain on an absolute legal equality with the others. Such an equality did in fact exist: each was entitled to two Senators in the Confederate Congress; the territory of each could not be altered without its consent; no state could enter singly into an alliance or treaty with a foreign country; each was guaranteed a republican form of government; full faith and credit were given in each to the public acts, records, and judicial proceedings of every other; the citizens of each were entitled to all the privileges and immunities of citizens in the others. These provisions continued to be implemented as they had been under Washington government, and there is no evidence to indicate any changes were initiated except those relating to the institution of slavery.

X

THE CONFEDERACY IN THEORY AND PRACTICE

Was this Confederacy a union of states which retained their sovereignty in full? Was there in reality a national existence apart from the separate existence of each state? And did the Confederacy become in practical terms a union of the the southern people as a whole? The available evidence supports the view that there was a union of the people and that the Confederacy satisfied the principal criteria which can be used to determine if a governmental system is "federal" in nature.

Observably, there was a division of power between the central government and the state governments. We can assume, moreover, that in 1861 the powers of external sovereignty passed to the Confederacy as a whole, although neither Lincoln's administration nor the United States Supreme Court would agree that it constituted a separate people or a nation state. Later in the war Jefferson Davis expressed a hope in communication with Lincoln that peace would soon be reached between the "two countries"; the northern President, declining to grant recognition to the Richmond government, replied that it was essential to unite our "common country."

But the point is that Confederate leaders believed they were leading a "nation" at war. Even though the south was too late in seceding, the 1787 Union came close to dissolution through force of arms, and it was only after the 1861-1865 conflict that the United States Supreme Court declared ours was an indestructible union of indestructible states. While the Lincoln government would not recognize the Confederacy as a separate country, the observable condition remains that for all practical purposes it was just that.

Of primary importance is the question concerning the placement of the powers of external sovereignty during these years. Palpably, it was the central government which sought foreign recognition; while its efforts were nugatory, they were made by Richmond and not by the individual states as such. The Confederate government exercised the powers to declare war, conclude peace and implement foreign policies. However ineffectual its efforts might have been, the relevance is these powers constitute the desiderata of external sovereignty. As Lincoln learned to realize from experience, these powers did not remain with the Union, and they definitely did not reside in the individual Confederate state, even if it theoretically had retained its sovereignty in full under the 1861 Constitution.

If the powers of external sovereignty passed directly from the British Crown in 1776 to the American people as a whole, then they must have passed to the southern people as a whole in 1861. If these powers had been transferred to the national government under the 1787 document, even if they were not mentioned in it, then the same principle must assign them to the central government under the Confederacy. And if these powers were implemented by Richmond, the presumption must be that the states did not retain their sovereignty intact. If this was the situation, then sovereignty must have been divided by someone, and the "someone" was the people taken as a whole body politic. As was the case in the federal Union, this argument corroborates the viewpoint that the Confederacy was a union of people rather than one of sovereign states.

Although the general government was granted powers of substance in internal matters, the constitutional division of powers between the central and state governments could not be altered unilaterally by Richmond. Significantly, the Confederate government was directly in contact with citizens as individuals and not just as members of their state body politics. The central government secured authority from individuals *per se* through the election of officials to the executive and legislative branches of the government; it directly imposed taxes on them and had direct contact with them through securing their obedience to its own laws. As Webster pointed out, no closer relationship can exist between an individual and his government than when the latter taxes and drafts him for military service. Manifestly, Confederate citizens had to give a fidelity to both Richmond and their state governments; its meaning was that a "national citizenship" apart from that in any state did exist and that a dual citizenship status was present.

Relevant constitutional provisions made the general government supreme within its own sphere of action, and when the government expanded its powers beyond the intent of the Montgomery framers, it could exert its supremacy over conflicting state laws and actions. Under express sections of the Constitution the states were granted reserved powers, all powers not delegated to the central government nor prohibited by the fundamental law to the states being reserved to them or to their peoples. But when Richmond exceeded its constitutional powers, the presumption can only be that the government encroached on these reserved rights. It is demonstrable that the government did not remain within the strict legal limits assigned to it by the Constitution, and when it exceeded these limits, its actions were judicially sustained. As a general rule, the states were not used to administer "national" programs, for Richmond used its own officials or exerted supervisory control over state personnel in implementing national policies.

Just as the general government became active in a way unforeseen by the framers, so also did the state governments assume a more positive role in the economic and political process. Clearly, matters given them as constituent units were substantial, as they imposed their own taxes, secured compliance with their own laws and regulations, and generally exercised autonomy within their own sphere of action. They were at liberty to design their own forms of government and procedure, and they were assured constitutionally of an absolute equality with one another.

In practice, then, the Confederacy was a union of the people as a whole, and sovereignty or supreme political authority resided in individuals *per se;* through them sovereignty was in effect divided between the nation and the states. That the 1861 Constitution did not represent a "compact" among sovereign states was certain, for it constituted the union of a people.

It is not comprehensible why Americans of a century ago were preoccupied with the locus of sovereignty, because in both the Union and the Confederacy the central and state governments were working partners in an on-going system. Even if there is a division of sovereignty in a body politic, the result need not be an irreconcilable conflict between the general and state governments. While there can be conflict, the emphasis can also be put on co-operative action between the general and state governments.

The struggle that was part of the Confederate experience demonstrated the new governmental system was functioning: to say that the system was weak because conflict existed is to overlook an integral element in the political process. The system was workable and adaptable to new conditions — it would have been unusual if no struggle for power had existed between Richmond and the state governments. Whatever the theory, the Confederacy proved to be activist and viable, the principal reason being that it had taken on most of the features of the "federal" system as practiced in the Union.

2

There are some implications that can be taken from the experience of more than a century ago. That the war itself fostered the evolution of an active central government was evident, for Richmond could not afford to assume a *laissez faire* attitude toward involvement in the economy and in the lives of individual citizens. To support military operations, "national" resources had to be mobilized; when the government entered novel areas of governmental control, it could find support in constitutional provisions sustaining its actions. Early in the nineteenth century Chief Justice Marshall of the United States Supreme Court suggested that the 1787 document was adaptable enough to meet various crises in human affairs: the Confederate Constitution, largely a copy of the older one, revealed equal adaptability in confronting new challenges.

Generally speaking, the 1861 document granted powers to the central government that favored its taking a dominant attitudinal approach to the processes of government. To say that the framers would have been well advised to have drafted an entirely new basic law which would have more expressly indicated their philosophy seems credible. If the Confederate framers had wanted to make sure the general government would be a limited one under which the states would retain their sovereignty, they could have copied the Confederation Articles. Since Richmond was granted an extensive range of powers corroborated by a supremacy clause, how could it have been kept within rigid legal limits? Basically, the difficulty was that the Montgomery Constitution was "structured" against the concept of state sovereignty and rights.

In considering the liberal divergencies between constitutional theory and practice the point that stands out is that the legal base supporting the institution of slavery remained unaltered through more than four years of war. What this circumstance suggests is that the primary reason for secession was a determination to find a permanent protection for slavery, whose legal status was open to doubt under the Washington government.

Obviously, the south had other subsidiary complaints against the north for its alleged wrongdoing. Its spokesmen had complained that the protective tariff had had a deleterious effect on an agricultural economy; yet once withdrawal came, they too revealed an interest in a high tariff to safeguard a nascent industry. Also, leaders had complained that the north had benefited disproportionately through internal improvement programs of the federal government; still, during the conflict Richmond undertook activities that indicated the central government would meet demands for improvements having a domestic ramification. They had complained about the "consolidationists," who wanted to see a centralized national government in Washington, but they created in their own image a general government of similar power, prestige and authority.

3

Briefly, we might discuss what might have happened to the Confederacy if its people had won independence. In that generation succeeding the Civil War, the Richmond government would doubtless have come to resemble the Washington government more and more. The years from 1865 to 1900 would have been given to rebuilding the country's economic-political system, and in this process of reconstruction the central government would have had again to take an activist role. What had been necessary in war would have been no less essential in peace. Because reconstruction would have necessitated a government of greater resources and power, the individual states would have been hard put to accomplish what had to be done.

It is reasonable to assume that other changes would have taken place. For instance, the nascent industry which began to evolve during the 1850's would have required the support of government, and one result might have been that southerners would have given a more favorable consideration to a protective tariff policy. In all probability changes would have been forthcoming in the Confederate document to make it even more adaptable to new circumstances. A Supreme Court would undoubtedly have been established, and a high court, as the United States Court before it, would have given its sanction to the assertion of national powers and responsibilities.

There is cause to believe a workable two-party system would have developed; the old centralist-decentralist arguments would have continued since the economic, social and political conditions which stimulated these controversies would have been present again. There would have been contention between the old Whig element, espousing the interests of a central government, and the states' righters, favoring a government of limited objective.

It is questionable that various parliamentary features of the 1861 Constitution would have been any more successful of implementation in peace than they were in war. It is even more debatable that slavery would have been abolished until the end of the century, if then; the prime field hand was still worth a considerable sum in 1860, and any facile assumption that general emancipation would have followed the conflict's end is unwarrantable.

Where would the powers of external sovereignty have resided after the war? They would have been retained by the general government, where they remained in practice from 1861 to 1865. Recognition of the central government by European and other countries would have granted the Confederacy a status in the contemporary international family of nations, and its position as a separate nation state would have been confirmed further. In the event of recognition this "union" of the southern people would have become both a *practical* and *legal* fact.

Of course, theory and practice can not be fully consistent one with the other. Several of the Confederate states had been among the original thirteen colonies; their leaders, especially the Virginians, had been influential in the initial years of the United States government. Yet one of these opinion-makers, Jefferson, when once in office, avoided a strict construction of the 1787 Constitution, and for their own part articulators of the Confederacy could not put into practice what they advocated in theory.

Finally, it is unlikely that any independent Confederate experience beyond 1865 would have led to major departures from American constitutionalism in theory or practice. And it is debatable if this experiment at self-government can be considered a genuine deviation from our total constitutional development.

In the sixties of this century the central government of the Confederacy, if still existing, would have had to exert national rights and assert nation-wide responsibilities affecting all its citizens. And it would have been confronted by the same congeries of national-state problems which the United States is now experiencing.

REFERENCES

CHAPTER 1

1. A. C. McLaughlin, *A Constitutional History of the United States*, p. 135.
2. J. L. M. Curry, *Civil History of the Government of the Confederate States*.
3. W. F. Dodd, *Cases and Materials on Constitutional Law*, p. 443.
4. Louis Pendleton, *Alexander H. Stephens*, p. 189.
5. A. H. Stephens, *A Constitutional View of the Late War Between the States*, vol. 1.
6. *Ibid.*, vol. 2
7. Jefferson Davis, *The Rise and Fall of the Confederate Government*, vol. 1.
8. Stephens, *op. cit.*, vol. 1.   9. J. B. McMaster, *Daniel Webster*, p. 215.
10. Davis, *op. cit.*
11. A. O. Spain, *The Political Theory of John C. Calhoun*, p. 49.
12. *Ibid.*
13. J. M. Mathews, *The American Constitutional System*, p. 62.
14. A. W. MacMahon, *ed.*, *Federalism: Mature and Emergent*, pp. 4-5.
15. J. D. Richardson, *ed.*, *A Compilation of the Messages and Papers of the Confederacy*, vol. 1, p. 33.
16 Davis, *op. cit.*   17. Richardson, *op.cit.*, p. 185.
18. W. F. McCaleb, *ed.*, *Memoirs of J. H. Reagan*, p. 91.
19. McLaughlin, *op. cit.*, pp. 611-612.

CHAPTER II

1. Davis, *op. cit.*
2. Robert McElroy, *Jefferson Davis: The Unreal and the Real*, vol. 2, p. 264.
3. E. M. Coulter, *The Confederate States of America, 1861-1865*, p. 21.
4. McElroy, *op. cit.*, p. 263.   5. Curry, *op. cit.*   6. Davis, *op. cit.*
7. W. M. Robinson, *Justice in Grey*, p. 622.   8. Davis, *op. cit.*

CHAPTER III

1. Davis, *op. cit.*, vol. 1, p. 205.
2. H. .J Eckenrode, *Jefferson Davis: President of the South*, p. 111.
3. Davis, *op. cit.*, p. 207.   4. McCaleb, *op. cit.*, *p.* 123.
5: Clement Eaton, *A History of the Southern Confederacy*, p. 47.
6. Eckenrode, *op. cit.*, p. 123.
7. R. W. Patrick, *Jefferson and His Cabinet*, p. 58.
8. Pierce Butler, *Judah P. Benjamin*, p. 230.   9. Coulter, *op. cit.*, p. 198.
10. H. A. Trexler, "Jefferson Davis and the Confederate Patronage," *South Atlantic Quarterly* (January, 1929), vol. 28, pp. 45-58.
11. Trexler, *op. cit.*, p. 56.
12. J. T. Durkin, *Stephen R. Mallory: Confederate Navy Chief*, p. 176.
13. McCaleb, *op. cit.*, p. 120.   14. F. E. Vandiver, *Rebel Brass*, p. 43.
15. *Ibid.*, p. 30.   16. Patrick, *op. cit.*, p. 128.
17. *The War of the Rebellion*, Series IV, vol. 3, pp. 1046-1047.

18. Richardson, *op. cit.*, vol. 1, p. 75.

19. Elisabeth Cutting, *Jefferson Davis: Political Soldier*, p. 183.

20. B. J. Hendrick, *Statesmen of the Lost Cause*, p. 429.

21. J. C. Schwab, *The Confederate States of America, 1861-1865*, p. 186.

22. Robinson, *op. cit.*, pp. 397-398.   23. Trexler, *op. cit.*, p. 53.

24. R. S. Henry, *The Story of the Confederacy*, p. 76.

25. *Ibid.*, p. 389.

26. A. B. Moore, *Conscription and Conflict in the Confederacy*, p. 340.

27. Coulter, *op. cit.*, p. 270.

28. T. R. Hay, "The South and the Arming of the Slaves," *Mississippi Valley Historical Review* (June, 1919), vol. 6, pp. 34-73.

29. C. H. Wesley, *The Collapse of the Confederacy*, p. 162.

30. R. G. Cleland, " Jefferson Davis and the Confederate Congress," *Southeastern Historical Quarterly* (January, 1916), vol. 19, pp. 213-231.

31. Wesley, *op. cit.*, p. 89.   32. Patrick, *op. cit.*, pp. 74-75.

33. Eaton, *op. cit.*, p. 58.   34. Richardson, *op. cit.*, p. 400.

35. *Ibid.*, p. 324.

36. *Journal of the Congress of the Confederate States of America*, vol. 5, p. 107.

37. Richardson, *op. cit.*, p. 160.

38. J. B. McMaster, *A History of the People of the United States during Lincoln's Administration*, p. 575.   39. *Journal, op. cit.*, vol. 4, p. 727.

CHAPTER IV

1. E. A. Pollard, *The Last Year of the War*, p. 177.

2. J. W. DuBose, *The Life and Times of W. L. Yancey*, vol. 2, p. 678.

3. Eaton, *op. cit.*, p. 55.   4. Patrick, *op. cit.*, p. 75.

5. *Acts and Resolutions of the First Session of the Provisional Congress of the Confederate States*, p. 68.

6. *Acts and Resolutions of the Second Session, op. cit.*, p. 8.

7. *Acts and Resolutions of the Fourth Session, op. cit.*, p. 102.

8. James M. Matthews, ed., *Public Laws of the Confederate States of America, First Session, First Congress*, p. 1.

9. *Proceedings of the First Confederate Congress*, vol. 47, pp. 82-85.

10. Matthews, *op. cit.*, pp. 30-31.

11. *Proceedings, op. cit.*, vol. 45, pp. 26-27.

12. *Proceedings, op. cit.*, vol. 46, pp. 44-208.   13. *Ibid.*, pp. 139-140.

14. DuBose, *op. cit.*, p. 682.   15. *Proceedings, op. cit.*, vol. 48, p. 4.

16. *Ibid.*, pp. 14-319.   17. *Ibid.*, vol. 50, p. 68.

18. Matthews, *op. cit.*, p. 33.   19. *Ibid.*, p. 38.

20. R. C. Black, *The Railroads of the Confederacy*, pp. 121 and 280.

21. *Journal, op. cit.*, p. 443.   22. *Proceedings, op. cit.*, pp. vii and 269.

23. Henry, *op. cit.*, p. 445.   24. Matthews, *op. cit.*, p. 2.

25. Matthews, *Public Laws, op. cit., Third Session, First Congress*, p. 102.

26. Matthews, *Public Laws, op cit., Fourth Session, First Congress*, pp. 188-189.

27. *Proceedings,* op. cit., vol. 50, p. 340.

28. *Ibid.*, pp. 129-131.   29. Matthews, *op. cit.*, p. 235.

30. *Journal of the Congress of the Confederate States of America, 1861-1865*, vol. 7, p. 442.

CHAPTER V

1. *Acts and Resolutions of the First Session of the Provisional Congress of the Confederate States*, pp. 64-65.
2. H. D. Capers, *The Life and Times of C. G. Memminger*, p. 340.
3. R. C. Todd, *Confederate Finance*, p. 31.
4. W. J. Shultz and M. R. Caine, *Financial Development of the United States*, p. 276.

5. Patrick, *op. cit.*, p. 212.
6. Schwab, *op. cit.*, p. 9.
7. Todd, *op. cit.*, p. 136.
8. Capers, *op. cit.*, p. 342.
9. Schwab, *op. cit.*, p. 18.
10. Richardson, *op. cit.*, vol. 1, p. 235.
11. Todd, *op. cit.*, p. 118.
12. Schwab, *op. cit.*, p. 89.
13. Todd, *op. cit.*, p. 68.
14. Richardson, *op. cit.*, p. 293.
15. Schwab, *op. cit.*, p. 46.
16. Richardson, *op. cit.*, p. 361.
17. Todd, *op. cit.*, pp. 72-73.
18. Capers, *op. cit.*, p. 344.
19. Schwab, *op. cit.*, p. 98.
20. Coulter, *op. cit.*, p. 170.
21. Schwab, *op. cit.*, p. 248.
22. *Ibid.*, p. 248.
23. *Acts and Resolutions of the First Session . . .*, p. 58.
24. Todd, *op. cit.*, p. 130.
25. Patrick, *op. cit.*, p. 336.
26. Richardson, *op. cit.*, p. 336.
27. Todd, *op. cit.*, p. 152.
28. McCaleb, *op. cit.*, p. 113.
29. Todd, *op. cit.*, p. 37.
30. McCaleb., *op. cit.*, p. 113.
31. Schwab, *op. cit.*, p. 117.
32. *Ibid.*, p. 34.
33. Shultz and Caine, *op. cit.*, p. 285.
34. Richardson, *op. cit.*, p. 562.
35. Eaton, *op. cit.*, p. 251.

CHAPTER VI

1. *Acts and Resolutions of the First Session of the Provisional Congress of the Confederate States*, pp. 4-8.
2. W. F. McCaleb, "The Organization of the Post Office Department of the Confederacy," *American Historical Review* (October, 1906) vol. 12, p. 72.
3. F. B. C. Bradlee, *Blockade Running during the Civil War*, p. 278.
4. Black, *op. cit.*, p. 30.
5. Shultz and Caine, *op. cit.*, p. 272.
6. J. M. Matthews, *Public Laws of the Confederate States of America, First Session of the First Congress*, pp. 8-9.
7. *Act and Resolutions of the First Session of the Provisional Congress . . . op. cit.*, p. 13.
8. F. E. Vandiver, *Rebel Brass*, p. 86.
9. D. H. Hill, *Bethel to Sharpsburg . . .*, vol. 1, p. 120.
10. *Ibid.*, p. 134.
11. T. C. Bryan, *Confederate Georgia*, p. 24.
12. C. W. Ramsdell, "The Confederate Government and the Railroads," *American Historical Review* (July, 1917), vol. 22, p. 802.
13. C. W. Ramsdell, "The Control of Manufacturing by the Confederate Government," *Mississippi Valley Historical Review* (December, 1921), vol. 8. p. 235.
14. *Ibid.*, p. 236.
15. Vandiver, *Ploughshares into Swords*, op. cit., pp. 161-162.
16. *Ibid.*, p. 162.
17. Bradlee, *op. cit.*, p. 168.
18. R. L. Thompson, *Wiring a Continent*, p. 374.

19. W. F. Plum, *The Military Telegraph During the Civil War*, p. 135.
20. Ramsdell, *Behind the Lines* . . . , p. 283.
21. J. K. Bettersworth, *Confederate Mississippi*, p. 185.
22. *Ibid.*, p. 186.   23. Moore, *op. cit.*, p. 218.
24. *Ibid.*, pp. 191-234.
25. *The War of the Rebellion* . . . , Series IV, vol. 2, p. 724.
26. Moore, *op. cit.*, p. 323.   27. Bettersworth, *op. cit.*, p. 82.
28. Ramsdell, *Behind the Lines* . . . , p. 50.
29. Coulter, *op. cit.*, p. 252.
30. F. L. Owsley, *State Rights in the Confederacy*, p. 222.
31. J. D. Bragg, *Louisiana in the Confederacy*, p. 261.
32. J. W. Garner, *Reconstruction in Mississippi*, p. 24.
33. H. T. Lefler, ed., *North Carolina History Told By Contemporaries*, p. 294.
34 Hill, *op. cit.*, p. 329.
35. Ramsdell, *Behind the Lines* . . . , p. 94.
36. M. E. Massey, *Ersatz in the Confederacy*, p. 26.
37. Black, *op. cit.*, p. 206.   37. Black, *op. cit.*, p. 206.
38. Ramsdell, *op. cit.*, p. 97.   39. *Official Records*, op. cit., p. 724.
40. Capers, *op. cit.*, p. 487.   41. Henry, *op. cit.*, p. 93.

CHAPTER VII

1. Davis, *op cit.*, vol. 1, p. 259.
2. W. M. Robinson, "Legal System of the Confederate States," *Journal of Southern History* (November, 1938), vol. 4, p. 457.
3. Robinson, *Justice in Grey*, op. cit., p. 22.
4. J. M. Matthews, ed., *The Statutes at Large of the Provisional Government of the Confederate States of America*, pp. 77-86.
5. Robinson, *op. cit.*, pp. 57-58.   6. *Ibid.*, p. 423.
7. *Ibid.*, p. 424.
8. J. G. de Roulhac Hamilton, "The State Courts and the Confederate Constitution," *Journal of Southern History* (November, 1938), vol. 4, p. 430.
9. Moore, *op. cit.*, p. 162.
10. *Proceedings of the First Confederate Congress, op. cit.*, vol. 48, p. 40.
11. Moore, *op. cit.*, p. 164.   12. *Proceedings, op. cit.*, p. 324.
13. R. W. Patrick, *The Opinions of the Confederate Attorneys General, 1861-1865*, pp. xviii-xxi.
14. *Ibid.*, pp. 95-314.
15. *Official Records, op. cit.*, Series IV, vol. 3, p. 875.
16. *Ibid.*, pp. 875-880.   17. *Ibid.*, pp. 877-878.
18. Durkin, *op. cit.*, p. 330.   19. Moore, *op. cit.*, p. 163.
20. Patrick, *Jefferson Davis, op. cit.*, p. 308.
21. Hendrick, *op. cit.*, p. 413.
22. W. A. Dunning, *Studies in Southern History and Politics*, p. 111.
23. Dunning, *op. cit.*, p. 110.   24. *Ibid.*, p. 113.
25. Hamilton, *op. cit.*, p. 436.   26. *Official Records*, op. cit., p. 891.
27. Dunning, *op. cit.*, pp. 123-126.   28. Hamilton, *op. cit.*, p. 447.
29. Dunning, *op. cit.*, p. 133.

CHAPTER VIII

1. *Official Records, op. cit.,* Series IV, vol. 1, p. 117.
2. C. S. Raines, *ed., Memoirs of Francis Richard Lubbock,* pp. 355-356.
3. *Moore, op. cit.,* p. 3.   4. D. H. Hill, *op. cit.,* vol. 1, p. 181.
5. E. M. Coulter, *A Short History of Georgia,* p. 309.
6. Henry, *op. cit.,* p. 125.   7. Moore, *op. cit.,* p. 231.
8. Davis, *op. cit.,* pp. 507-657.   9. *Ibid.,* pp. 511-512.
10. L. B. Hill, *op. cit.,* p. 82.   11. *Official Records, op. cit.,* p. 1128.
12. Moore, *op. cit.,* p. 283.
13. *Official Records,* Series IV, vol. 2, p. 74.
14. Raines, *op. cit.,* p. 472.   15. Moore, *op. cit.,* p. 232.
16. *Ibid.,* p. 236.   17. Stephens, *op. cit.,* vol. 2, p. 572.
18. Moore, *op. cit.,* p. 262.   19. Coulter, *op. cit.,* p. 317.
20. Bryan, *op. cit.,* p. 88.   21. Schwab, *op. cit.,* p. 201.
22. *Official Records,* op. cit., p. 131.
23. W. L. Fleming, *Civil War and Reconstruction in Alabama,* p. 89.
24. Moore, *op. cit.,* p. 241.   25. Bettersworth, *op. cit.,* p. 75.
26. Moore, *op. cit.,* p. 75.   27. *Ibid.,* pp. 269-270.
28. Allen Tate, *Jefferson Davis: His Rise and Fall,* pp. 255-256.
29. Moore, *op. cit.,* pp. 278-279.   30. Hill, *op cit.,* p. 231.
31. D. Y. Thomas, *Arkansas in War and Reconstruction,* p. 320.
32. Robinson, *op. cit.,* p. 412.
33. R. M. Johnston and W. H. Browne, *Life of Alexander H. Stephens,* p. 422.
34. U. B. Phillips, *ed., Annual Report of the American Historical Association for the Year 1911,* p. 633.
35. Bryan, *op. cit.,* p. 96.   36. Hill, *op. cit.,* p. 206.
37. Schwab, *op. cit.,* pp. 192-199.   38. Moore, *op. cit.,* p. 287-288.
39. *Ibid.,* p. 287-288.   40. Todd, *op. cit.,* p. 170.
41. W. W. Davis, *op. cit.,* pp. 191, 216.
42. Bragg, *op. cit.,* pp. 261-262.
43. L. B. Hill, *State Socialism in the Confederate States of America,* pp. 10, 14.
44. Todd, *op. cit.,* p. 191.   45. Hill, *op. cit.,* p. 20.
46. Richardson, *op. cit.,* p. 509.
47. R. E. Yates, "Governor Vance and the Peace Movement," *North Carolina Historical Review* (January, 1940), vol. 17, p. 15.
48. *Official Records,* vol. 2, p. 795.   49. Schwab, *op. cit.,* p. 225.
50. Wesley, *op. cit.,* p. 67.   51. Coulter, *op. cit.,* p. 293.

CHAPTER IX

1. Eaton, *op. cit.,* p. 267.
2. L. A. Kibler, *Benjamin F. Perry,* p. 354.
3. K. A. Hanna, *Florida: Land of Change,* p. 274.
4. Hamilton, *Reconstruction in North Carolina,* p. 39.
5. Garner, *op. cit.,* p. 43.   6. *Ibid.,* p. 48.
7. Bragg, *op. cit.,* p. 228.   8. Bettersworth, *op. cit.,* p. 73.
9. Emmett Kilpatrick, *The Political History of Alabama during the War of Secession,* p. 117.

10. W. W. Davis, "The Civil War and Reconstruction in Florida," p. 220.

11. Bettersworth, *op. cit.*, p. 40.   12. Garner, *op. cit.*, p. 39.

13. Bettersworth, *op. cit.*, p. 37.   14. Bragg, *op. cit.*, p. 201.

15. Bryan, *op. cit.*, p. 48.   16. *Bragg, op. cit.*, p. 186.

17. Bryan, *op. cit.*, p. 61.   18. Hamilton, *op. cit.*, p. 77.

19. Bragg, *op. cit.*, p. 194.   20. *Ibid.*, p. 238.